D1559927

ANSI/ASQC Q90/ISO 9000 GUIDELINES FOR USE BY THE CHEMICAL AND PROCESS INDUSTRIES

Also available from Quality Press

Quality Assurance for the Chemical and Process Industries—A Manual of Good Practices
ASQC Chemical and Process Industries Division Chemical Interest Committee

ISO 9000 Equivalent: ANSI/ASQC Q90–1987 Series—Quality Management and Quality Assurance Standards

To request a complimentary 80-page catalog of publications, call 800-952-6587.

ANSI/ASQC Q90/ISO 9000 GUIDELINES FOR USE BY THE CHEMICAL AND PROCESS INDUSTRIES

**ASQC Chemical and Process Industries Division
Chemical Interest Committee**

ASQC Quality Press
Milwaukee, Wisconsin

ANSI/ASQC Q90/ISO 9000 GUIDELINES FOR USE BY THE CHEMICAL AND PROCESS INDUSTRIES

ASQC Chemical and Process Industries Division
Chemical Interest Committee

Library of Congress Cataloging-in-Publication Data

ANSI/ASQC Q90/ISO 9000 : guidelines for use by the chemical and
   process industries / ASQC Chemical and Process Industries
   Division, Chemical Interest Committee.
      p.   cm.
   ISBN 0-87389-196-1
   1. Chemical industry—Quality control—Standards. I. American
Society for Quality Control. Chemical Interest Committee.
TP149.A6 1992
660'.021873—dc20   91-43867
                                                        CIP

10 9 8 7 6 5 4 3 2 1

ISBN 0-87389-196-1

Acquisitions Editor: Jeanine L. Lau
Production Editor: Mary Beth Nilles
Marketing Administrator: Susan Westergard
Set in Gamma by DanTon Typographers. Cover design by Artistic License. Printed and bound by
BookCrafters.

For a free copy of the ASQC Quality Press publications catalog, including
ASQC membership information, call 800-952-6587.

Printed in the United States of America

 Printed on recycled paper

ASQC
Quality Press
611 East Wisconsin Avenue
Milwaukee, Wisconsin 53202

CONTENTS

PREFACE

The Chemical Interest Committee (CIC) of the Chemical and Process Industries Division of the American Society for Quality Control (ASQC) has prepared these guidelines. The intent is to provide guidance in using the American National Standard ANSI/ASQC Q91–1987 (ISO 9001) and to promote the use of Q90–Q94 standards in the chemical and process industries. In addition, these guidelines contain examples and good quality practices which may aid in developing effective quality assurance systems.

These guidelines are not intended to be used as a supplemental standard or to modify or alter the standard in any way.

The CIC developed these guidelines in cooperation with the Total Quality Council of the Chemical Manufacturers Association's CHEMSTAR Division.

The CIC acknowledges the use of resource materials provided by the following organizations:

> International Organization for Standardization (ISO), Technical Committee on Quality Assurance (TC–176) *Quality Management and Quality Assurance Standards – Part 2: Generic Guideline for Application of ISO 9001, ISO 9002, ISO 9003, ISO/CD 9000-2*

> ASQC Chemical and Process Industries Division, CIC, *Quality Assurance for the Chemical and Process Industries—A Manual of Good Practices*

> Chemical Industry Association, London, England, *ISO 9001. EN 29001, BS 5750:Part 1:1987: Guidelines for Use by the Chemical and Allied Industries*

ACKNOWLEDGMENTS

The CIC appreciates the continuing support and encouragement of the Total Quality Council of the Chemical Manufacturers Association's CHEMSTAR Division.

CIC members to be acknowledged for their contributions to these guidelines are:

Jim Bigelow	Rudy Kittlitz
Frank Bondurant	Norman Knowlden
Bradford Brown	James Krueger
Georgia Kay Carter	Perce Ness
Don Engelstad	Bill Ochs
David Files	Chris Ostman
Peter Fortini	Anil Parikh
Dwight Grimestad	Philip Parker
Richard Hoff (chair)	Frank Sinibaldi
	Jack Weiler

The following companies' support is hereby acknowledged.

Al–Jubail Petrochemical Co.
Allied–Signal Inc.
American Cyanamid Co.
Bradford S. Brown, Consultant–Quality and Statistics
Champion International Corp.
Dow Corning Corp.
Du Pont
Eastman Kodak Co.
Exxon Chemical Co.
Hercules Incorporated
Monsanto Chemical Co.
Nalco Chemical Co.
Occidental Chemical Corp.
Omni Tech International, Ltd.
Quantum Chemical Corp.
Shell Chemical Co.

The committee would like to acknowledge Donna Foco of Omni Tech International, Ltd. for her administrative support.

INTRODUCTION

PURPOSE

If your company is in a chemical or process industry (CPI), this guide will help you apply the national quality system models, ANSI/ASQC Q90-94-1987. Hereafter referenced as Q90, Q91, Q92, Q93, or Q94. This system directly matches the international quality system known as ISO 9000-9004. There are at least two reasons for using this guide:

- It includes activities that bear directly or indirectly on the quality of your products and services (e.g., quality planning, procedures, training, audits, system reviews, and documentation).

- It provides useful interpretation of the meaning of Q91 (ISO 9001) for the chemical and process industries. Q91 originally focused on mechanical industries, and some provisions require interpretation in CPI terms.

PRINCIPAL CONCEPTS

Organizations seek to accomplish three objectives with regard to quality:

- To achieve and sustain the quality of products and services that continually meets the purchaser's stated or implied needs

- To support management's confidence that the intended quality is being achieved and sustained

- To instill confidence in the purchaser that the intended quality is being, or will be, achieved

HISTORY

The International Organization for Standardization (ISO) issued the ISO 9000 series documents in 1987. Although they were the first quality-related guidelines published by ISO, they broke no new ground. Rather, they distilled tried and proven quality practices. What made them instantly attractive was that they had been approved by many nations. They were a comprehensive set of *standards and guidelines* for a quality system. ISO intended that they would be used as standards by the marketplace, where purchasers would write contracts requiring suppliers to meet the provisions of 9001, 9002, or 9003.

In 1987 the United States adopted an identical set of standards using American terms.

The United Kingdom has adopted the same standards as BS5750 and many other countries have endorsed the same, or similar, standards under various designations. A partial list appears in Figure I-1 on page xiii.

Officials in the European community saw that the ISO guidelines could set common standards for the quality of materials produced in any member country. They adopted the ISO guidelines as EN 29000–29004.

In summary, this quality model has received broad worldwide support.

THE STANDARDS

The five documents in the Q90 series are a linked set. The ISO 9000 series has an identical linkage.

- Q90 (ISO 9000) is titled *Quality Management and Quality Assurance Standards: Guidelines for Selection and Use.* It sets forth the principal quality concepts, describes the use of these Standards within purchaser/supplier contracts, and provides *guidance* in the use of the other four Standards.

- Q91–Q93 (ISO 9001–9003) are Standards for quality systems that a purchaser may contractually require a supplier to meet. These Standards are suitable for use in external second party quality assurance agreements.

  — Q91 is the most comprehensive. It is appropriate when the contract calls for the supplier to *develop, design, produce, install, service, and supply* a product or service. All of the requirements of the other two Standards (Q92 and Q93) are included in Q91. *This guide focuses on Q91.*

  — Q92 is most appropriate when the contract calls for the supplier to *produce and supply* to an existing design. This guide will note which parts do not apply to Q92.

  — Q93 applies when the supplier is required to supply based only on final *inspection* and *testing.* This guide will note which parts do not apply to Q93.

- Q94, in contrast to Q91–Q93, is a guideline for *internal quality management* activities. This includes a set of quality elements which any company can use to develop its own internal quality system. A company which uses the practices discussed in Q94 should easily be able to meet a purchaser's requirement for compliance with Q91–Q93.

Standards Body	Quality management and quality assurance standards: Guidelines for selection and use	Quality systems: model for quality assurance in design/development, production, installation, and servicing	Quality systems: model for quality assurance in production and installation	Quality systems: model for quality assurance in final inspection and test	Quality management and quality system elements: guidelines
ISO	ISO 9000: 1987	ISO 9001: 1987	ISO 9002: 1987	ISO 9003: 1987	ISO 9004: 1987
Australia	AS 3900	AS 3901	AS 3902	AS 3903	AS 3904
Austria	OE NORM-PREN 29000	OE NORM-PREN 29001	OE NORM-PREN 29002	OE NORM-PREN 29003	OE NORM-PREN 29004
Belgium	NBN X 50-002-1	NBN X 50-003	NBN X 50-004	NBN X 50-005	NBN X 50-002-2
Canada	CSA Z299.0-88	CSA Z299.1-85	CSA Z299.2-85	CSA Z299.3-85	CSA Q420-87
China	GB/T 10300.1-88	GB/T 10300.2-88	GB/T 10300.3-88	GB/T 10300.4-88	GB/T 10300.5-88
Denmark	DS/EN 29000	DS/EN 29001	DS/EN 29002	DS/EN 29003	DS/EN 29004
European Community	EN 29000-1987	EN 29001-1987	EN 29002-1987	EN 29003-1987	EN 29004-1987
Finland	SFS-ISO 9000	SFS-ISO 9001	SFS-ISO 9002	SFS-ISO 9003	SFS-ISO 9004
France	NF X 50-121	NF X 50-131	NF X 50-132	NF X 50-133	NF X 50-122
Germany	DIN ISO 9000	DIN ISO 9001	DIN ISO 9002	DIN ISO 9003	DIN ISO 9004
Hungary	MI 18990-1988	MI 18991-1988	MI 18992-1988	MI 18993-1988	MI 18994-1988
India	IS: 10301 Part 2	IS: 10201 Part 4	IS: 10201 Part 5	IS: 10201 Part 6	IS: 10201 Part 3
Ireland	IS 300 Part 0 /ISO 9000	IS 300 Part 1 /ISO 9001	IS 300 Part 2 /ISO 9002	IS 300 Part 3 /ISO 9003	IS 300 Part 0 /ISO 9004
Italy	UNI/EN 29000-1987	UNI/EN 29001-1987	UNI/EN 29002-1987	UNI/EN 29003-1987	UNI/EN 29004-1987
Malaysia	—	MA 985/ISO 9001-1987	MS 985/ISO 9002-1987	MS 985/ISO 9003-1987	—
Netherlands	NEN-ISO 9000	NEN-ISO 9001	NEN-ISO 9002	NEN-ISO 9003	NEN-ISO 9004
New Zealand	NZS 5600: Part 1-1987	NZS 5601-1987	NZS 5602-1987	NZS 5603-1987	NZS 5600: Part 2-1987
Norway	NS-EN 29000: 1988	NS-EN 29001: 1988	NS-ISO 9002	NS-ISO 9003	—
South Africa	SABS 9157: Part 0	SABS 9157: Part I	SABS 0157: Part II	SABS 0157: Part III	SABS 0157: Part IV
Spain	UNE 66 900	UNE 66 901	UNE 66 902	UNE 66 903	UNE 66 904
Sweden	SS-1I0 9000: 1988	SS-ISO 9001: 1988	SS-ISO 9002: 1988	SS-ISO 9003: 1988	SS-ISO 9004: 1988
Switzerland	SN-ISO 9000	SN-ISO 9001	SS-ISO 9002	SN-ISO 9003	SN-ISO 9004
Tunisia	NT 110.18-1987	NT 110.19-1987	NT 110.20-1987	NT 110.21-1987	NT 110.22-1987
United Kingdom	BS 5750: 1987: Part 0: Section 0.1 ISO 9000/EN 29000	BS 5750: 1987: Part 1: ISO 9001/EN 29001	BS 5750: 1987: Part 2: ISO 9002/EN 29002	BS 5750: 1987: Part 3: ISO 9003/EN 29003	BS 5750: 1987: Part 0: Sec. 0.2 ISO 9004/EN 29004
USA	ANSI/ASQC Q90-1987	ANSI/ASQC Q91-1987	ANSI/ASQC Q92-1987	ANSI/ASQC Q93-1987	ANSI/ASQC Q94-1987
USSR	—	40.9001-88	40.9002-88	—	—
Yugoslavia	JUS A.K. 1.010	JUS A.K. 1.012	JUS A.K. 1.013	JUS A.K. 1.014	JUS A.K. 1.011

Figure I-1 Quality Systems Standards Matrix

A cross-reference between the Q90 Series Standards is given in Figure I-2.

HOW TO USE THIS GUIDE

We have translated the Standard into language used by the CPI. The intent is to provide comprehensive coverage of all elements of the Standard, even though some parts may not appear to have relevance to all CPI companies. This guide does not interpret clauses 0.0, 1.0, 2.0, and 3.0 in the Standard. The information in these clauses is self-explanatory.

Note that the word *product* in the Standards always includes *services* as well.

Clause			Description	Corresponding Q94 Clause
Q91	Q92	Q93		
4.1	4.1	4.1	Management Responsibility	4
4.2	4.2	4.2	Quality System	5
4.3	4.3	NA	Contract Review	7
4.4	NA	NA	Design Control	8
4.5	4.4	4.3	Document Control	17
4.6	4.5	NA	Purchasing	9
4.7	4.6	NA	Purchaser Supplied Product	No Equivalent
4.8	4.7	4.4	Product Identification and Traceability	11.2
4.9	4.8	NA	Process Control	10, 11
4.10	4.9	4.5	Inspection and Testing	12
4.11	4.10	4.6	Inspection, Measuring, and Test Equipment	13
4.12	4.11	4.7	Inspection and Test Status	11.7
4.13	4.12	4.8	Control of Nonconforming Product	14
4.14	4.13	NA	Corrective Action	15
4.15	4.14	4.9	Handling, Storage, Packaging, and Delivery	16
4.16	4.15	4.10	Quality Records	17.3
4.17	4.16	NA	Internal Quality Audits	5.4
4.18	4.17	4.11	Training	18
4.19	NA	NA	Servicing	16.2
4.20	4.18	4.12	Statistical Techniques	20

Figure I-2   Q91–Q94 Cross-Reference

There are three special terms that are used consistently in the Standard. This guide uses these terms in the same sense as the Standard's authors intended. To avoid confusion, it will be worthwhile to become familiar with these terms (see Figure I-3 on page xvi):

- *Supplier* refers to the company (organization, plant, or division) establishing a quality assurance system and producing the product or service covered by the Standard. You, as the user of this guide, will frequently be the supplier.

- *Sub-contractor* refers to any provider of purchased products (e.g., raw materials, in-bound goods, utilities, or equipment) or services (e.g., maintenance or packaging) which come *into* the supplier's company (organization, plant, or process). Toll converters, contract warehouses, laboratories, packagers, calibration services, and repackagers are examples of sub-contractors, whether internal or external. Operations *internal* to a supplier company may be regarded as sub-contractors if they are *outside* the quality system defined by the supplier.

- *Purchaser* refers to the company receiving the supplier's products or services. The purchaser is the supplier's customer. The purchaser chooses the quality requirements that the supplier's quality assurance system needs to satisfy.

Other specialized terms for the Q90 series are given in the glossary. Within each section of this guide, the format used to provide the information is:

- Introduction

- The clause is stated verbatum in the box

- Discussion of CPI-specific issues and good quality practices relating to the element

- Interpretations of the clause requirements.

- Interpretation of "Notes" in a Standard. These footnotes are advisory and not mandatory.

- Important linkages between parts of the Standard.

- Cautions regarding "unwritten rules" and "helpful hints" based on insights from experienced users of these Standards.

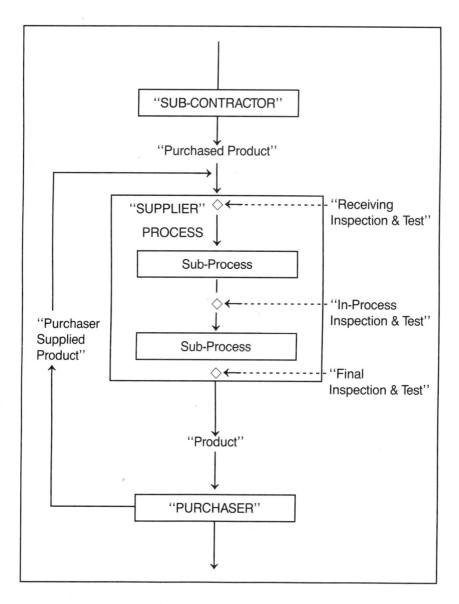

Figure I-3   ANSI/ASQC Q90/ISO 9000 Terminology

- Application of the guidance to related clauses in Q92 and Q93.

One of the Q91–Q93 Standards may be specifically referred to in contracts between a supplier and a purchaser.

The Standards are also used extensively as the basis for independent "third party" quality system registrations, although this was not the original intent. Registration is based on a comprehensive audit. The audit team should be competent in both this Standard and our industry's issues. It will look for objective evidence that your system is complete and effective. This may reduce the number of total audits your facility experiences. Registration may provide a marketing advantage.

The key to registration is the scope of the quality system as defined by the supplier. Internal suppliers must be considered when drafting the scope, since this will affect the breadth of the third party audit.

4.1 MANAGEMENT RESPONSIBILITY

INTRODUCTION: This clause of the Standard deals with senior management's leadership in and commitment to quality.

Q91-1987 Standard

4.1.1 Quality Policy

The supplier's management shall define and document its policy and objectives for, and commitment to, quality. The supplier shall insure that this policy is understood, implemented, and maintained at all levels in the organization.

GUIDANCE

The supplier's senior management shall develop a quality policy statement. The quality policy may also contain the mission, vision, and guidelines necessary to demonstrate the supplier's commitment to these values.

It is an unwritten rule that the policy statement should be signed and dated by the most senior executive, providing the first step in implementing the supplier's quality system (see clause 4.2). This policy should be a controlled document (see clause 4.5) and should be included in the quality manual. The supplier's management is responsible for communicating the quality policy throughout the organization and for reinforcing organization-wide ownership of the quality values through day-to-day actions.

Clause 4.1.1 in Q91 is identical to clause 4.1.1 in Q92. Clause 4.1.1 in Q93 only addresses defining a quality policy.

Q91–1987 Standard

4.1.2 Organization

4.1.2.1 Responsibility and Authority

The responsibility, authority, and the interrelation of all personnel who manage, perform, and verify work affecting quality shall be defined; particularly for personnel who need the organizational freedom and authority to:

   a) initiate action to prevent the occurrence of product nonconformity;

   b) identify and record any product quality problems;

   c) initiate, recommend, or provide solutions through designated channels;

   d) verify the implementation of solutions;

   e) control further processing, delivery, or installation of nonconforming product until the deficiency or unsatisfactory condition has been corrected.

GUIDANCE

Management should clearly define the responsibilities, authorities, and interfaces in the quality management system. Often a quality organization chart is used to show responsible functions and critical interfaces of personnel who carry out the activities identified in items (a) through (e). The quality organization chart need not duplicate the supplier's overall organization chart.

To facilitate document maintenance, the formal quality organization chart should not include individuals' names. However, it should refer to personnel documentation which can identify the current position holders.

Individuals responsible for quality-related actions must have the authority to take those actions in a timely and complete manner.

Clause 4.1.2.1 in Q91 is identical to clause 4.1.2.1 in Q92. Clause 4.1.2.1 in Q93 is limited to personnel engaged in final inspection and/or test.

Q91–1987 Standard

4.1.2.2 Verification Resources and Personnel

The supplier shall identify in-house verification requirements, provide adequate resources, and assign trained personnel for verification activities (see 4.18).

Verification activities shall include inspection, test, and monitoring of the design, production, installation, and servicing of the process and/or product; design reviews and audits of the quality system, processes, and/or product shall be carried out by personnel independent of those having direct responsibility for the work being performed.

GUIDANCE

The supplier should verify by laboratory test, process control data, subcontractor data, performance test, and/or inspection (see clause 4.10) that product meets specified requirements. In addition, the supplier should verify that production and other required activities conform to documented procedures.

The supplier should provide and schedule adequate space, equipment, facilities, and personnel for such verification work. Personnel who perform verification work must be independent of those being verified.

The supplier's management is required to assure that only trained personnel be assigned to test, inspection, product release, design review, and audit activities. Where such personnel are not available, the supplier should provide the required training (see clause 4.18).

The internal quality audit (see clause 4.17) is the major tool for the verification of the implementation and adequacy of procedures. Management representative (see clause 4.1.2.3) should provide adequate resources based on the frequency of audits. Some members of the audit team must represent functions other than those being audited.

Clause 4.1.2.2 in Q91 is substantially the same as clause 4.1.2.2 in

Q92 with the omission of design and servicing. Clause 4.1.2.2 in Q93 is limited to verification that product conforms to specified requirements.

Q91–1987 Standard

4.1.2.3 Management Representative

The supplier shall appoint a management representative who, irrespective of other responsibilities, shall have defined authority and responsibility for ensuring that the requirements of this Standard are implemented and maintained.

GUIDANCE

The supplier's management representative will generally be a high-ranking individual. The management representative may function as the quality assurance interface with the purchaser, sub-contractors, and external certifying bodies. The representative should oversee the supplier's compliance with all aspects of the Standard. The Standard does not require this person to devote full time to this responsibility as long as other assigned activities do not restrict the authority and opportunity to assure compliance with the Standard. Management representative may designate others to handle specific facets of the compliance program.

Clause 4.1.2.3 in Q92 and clause 4.1.2.3 in Q93 are identical to clause 4.1.2.3 in Q91.

Q91–1987 Standard

4.1.3 Management Review

The quality system adopted to satisfy the requirements of this Standard shall be reviewed at appropriate intervals by the supplier's management to ensure its continuing suitability and effectiveness. Records of such reviews shall be maintained (see 4.16).

NOTE: Management reviews normally include assessment of the results of internal quality audits, but are carried out by, or on behalf of, the supplier's management, namely management personnel having direct responsibility for the system (see 4.17).

GUIDANCE

This is one of the most important requirements of the Standard. Management must be involved in the quality system. This requires that management personnel conduct quality reviews.

Although it is not specifically required by the Standard, the supplier's management should formally review the operation of the entire quality system at least annually. When major changes to the quality system have been made, more frequent reviews may be required. Relevant statistical measures of quality and timeliness (see clause 4.20) should be presented as part of the review. Consider corrective actions (see clause 4.14) or redeployment of resources to remedy deficiencies. Records of the review (see clause 4.16) should include recommended actions. Subsequent reviews should examine the effectiveness of such actions.

Clause 4.1.3 is identical in Q91, Q92, and Q93.

The NOTE (which is not included in Q93) correctly states that internal audits provide valuable information for management reviews. However, the supplier's senior manager, not the quality assurance manager, should select a review panel including representatives from support functions (e.g., technical service, marketing, research, development, and finance), because changes in procedures or resources may be required for corrective action. The management representative (see clause 4.1.2.3) would be expected to coordinate the review meeting.

4.2 QUALITY SYSTEM

INTRODUCTION: This clause of the Standard defines the requirements for the supplier's quality system.

Q91–1987 Standard

4.2 Quality System

The supplier shall establish and maintain a documented quality system as a means of ensuring that product conforms to specified requirements. This shall include:

    a) the preparation of documented quality system procedures and instructions in accordance with the requirements of this Standard;

GUIDANCE

The Standard requires the supplier to have a documented quality system. Read Q94 clauses 4.4 to 5.3 for a complete discussion of quality systems. Two definitions from those clauses are cited:

*A quality system is the organizational structure, responsibilities, pro-
cedures, processes, and resources for implementing quality management.*

*The quality system typically applies to, and interacts with, all activities
pertinent to the quality of a product or service. It involves all phases
from initial identification to final satisfaction of requirements and
purchaser expectations.*

The scope of the quality system includes assuring the quality of both
product and service elements of the purchaser/supplier relationship.
The Q91 Standard states in clause 3.0 that the term "product" also
denotes "service" as appropriate. Thus, on-time delivery, correct invoicing,
and complaint resolution are also important.

The Standard requires that the quality system be documented,
demonstrating that a formal, organized quality system is in place and
providing an authoritative description of the system. An accepted method
of documenting the organization of a quality system is through a quality
manual. The quality manual is the directory of the quality system. It
should describe policy, specify responsibilities, and identify procedures.

The quality manual may be corporate or divisional, or it may describe
a specific process within a manufacturing site. It is important that the
quality manual define the scope of the quality system.

A documented quality system may use the concept of tiered documentation, the top tier of which is frequently the quality manual.
Occupying the lower tiers would be policies, procedures, and work
instructions and records.

As a minimum, the quality manual should address all the requirements in the Standard and any other standards related to quality systems
as appropriate for the industry and for the supplier (e.g., Good
Manufacturing Practices [GMP]). The manual also should refer to policies
and procedures related to:

- Specifications, including:
  — Raw materials
  — Process
  — Product
  — Package and label
  — Sales

- Safety system

- Purchaser service practices, including:
  — Order entry system
  — Product delivery system
  — Billing practices

- Purchaser relation practices, including:
  - Policy for sharing information
  - System for analyzing and resolving complaints
  - System for determining purchaser's needs

The Standard explicitly requires the supplier to document quality system procedures.

Q91–1987 Standard

4.2 Quality System

    b) the effective implementation of documented quality system procedures and instructions.

GUIDANCE

The quality system procedures and instructions should be effectively implemented, as evidenced by (for example):

- Internal quality audit reports

- Quantitative measures of performance

- Management reviews of the quality system

- Quality records

Q91–1987 Standard

4.2 NOTE: In meeting specified requirements, timely consideration needs to be given to the following activities:

GUIDANCE

Notes (a) through (g) point out items to consider before agreeing to supply product in accordance to the Q91 Standard. The supplier should decide the applicability of each note to a specific business.

Q91–1987 Standard

4.2 NOTE (*Continued*)

   a) The preparation of quality plans and a quality manual in accordance with specified requirements;

GUIDANCE

In practice, a quality manual has become a requirement for third party registration. In addition, internal and external audits are more effective with a quality manual as a reference. Note (a) also mentions the preparation of quality plans (see clause 4.4.2).

Quality plans may define how the quality requirements will be met for a contract, a class of products, or new products.

Other examples might include:

- Sampling plan

- Inspection plan

- New product plan

- Strategic quality system plan

A quality plan may include all the quality system elements; or it may cover only those parts of the quality system (specific procedures, testing, methods, and/or work instruction) that are added to or different from those required by the specific contract or class of products.

Q91–1987 Standard

4.2 NOTE (*Continued*)

b) the identification and acquisition of any controls, processes, inspection equipment, fixtures, total production resources, and skills that may be needed to achieve the required quality;

c) the updating, as necessary, of quality control, inspection, and testing techniques, including the development of new instrumentation;

d) the identification of any measurement requirement involving capability that exceeds the known state of the art in sufficient time for the needed capability to be developed;

e) the clarification of standards of acceptability for all features and requirements, including those which contain a subjective element;

f) the compatibility of the design, the production process, installation, inspection and test procedures, and the applicable documentation;

g) the identification and preparation of quality records (see 4.16).

GUIDANCE

In general, the notes describe the supplier's responsibility to be aware of the condition of processes affecting the quality of product or service. The notes also suggest the supplier should be aware of advances made in technology which could improve its processes. Finally, the notes imply that the supplier should carry out plans for controlling, evaluating, and improving its products, processes, and services, based upon the condition of its processes and available technology. Note that "processes" can be service, manufacturing, or business processes — virtually any process the supplier has within its company which can affect the quality of products or services.

Clause 4.2, Quality System, of the Q91 Standard is identical to Q92, clause 4.2 and is briefly summarized in Q93.

4.3 CONTRACT REVIEW

INTRODUCTION: This clause of the Standard covers the procedures a supplier uses to assure that it understands and is capable of meeting purchaser requirements.

Q91–1987 Standard

4.3 Contract Review

The supplier shall establish and maintain procedures for contract review and for the coordination of these activities.

Each contract shall be reviewed by the supplier to ensure that:

   a) the requirements are adequately defined and documented;

   b) any requirements differing from those in the tender are resolved;

   c) the supplier has the capability to meet contractual requirements.

continued

---

continued
Records of such contract reviews shall be maintained (see 4.16).

NOTE: The contract review activities, interfaces, and communication within the supplier's organization should be coordinated with the purchaser's organization, as appropriate.

GUIDANCE

The supplier must understand the purchasers' requirements and be able to meet contract requirements.

For purposes of this Standard, a contract can be either a formal document or an order received and accepted by the supplier. Contracts can cover:

- A single shipment

- Multiple shipments

- An order received against an annual forecasted volume

- A release against an annual contract

The supplier should have a system to ensure that:

- The purchasers' requirements are absolutely clear

- Any differences between the order and the original inquiry are resolved and agreed upon (that is, special customer requests are resolved)

- The terms and conditions of the order can be met as agreed

In reviewing and processing an order, several issues should be addressed:

- The essential features of each order (e.g., quantity, price, payment terms, specifications, packaging requirements, documentation, government regulations, and delivery points) need to be confirmed and transmitted to those who need the data to fill the order.

- The production schedule for multi-grade or multi-product plants must take into account stock levels, storage capacity, forecasted sales demand, and economic run length, as well as maintenance shutdowns.

- The point in the delivery process at which responsibility for maintaining the quality of product passes from the supplier to the purchaser or other party must be identified. In the case of consignment stocks, responsibility for the maintenance of quality needs to be defined and agreed upon in the contract.

- The supplier and purchaser must agree upon special purchaser requirements beyond the supplier's standard specification. The system or quality plan should ensure that such special requirements are known to all involved in processing the order.

- Contracts and orders are part of the documented quality system and should be controlled in the same manner as other records (see clause 4.16). In addition, the records of contract review should be maintained for each contract.

Meeting the needs of the purchaser requires systems and procedures that facilitate direct communication and teamwork among the sales, marketing, and manufacturing functions of the supplier.

The NOTE in the Standard applying to this clause is particularly valid for the chemical industry. Whenever appropriate, establish a dialogue between purchaser and supplier in regard to the purchaser's requirements.

For a product/service exchange agreement or contract, the parties need to define their respective responsibilities with regard to Q91 issues. All elements of Q91 should be considered in this purchaser/supplier exchange agreement.

This clause of Q91 is the same as clause 4.3 of Q92; it is not addressed in Q93.

4.4 DESIGN CONTROL

INTRODUCTION: This clause of the Standard should be referred to when the supplier takes a product or process design project under contract to a specific purchaser.

Q91–1987 Standard

4.4.1 General

The supplier shall establish and maintain procedures to control and verify the design of the product in order to ensure that the specified requirements are met.

GUIDANCE

Unless a research, development, process engineering, or facilities engineering design activity is being conducted under contract with a purchaser, the elements of this clause of the Standard are good quality practices to apply to design activities. Once uncontracted designs are complete, the results should be implemented into the quality system through process control (see clause 4.9.1) and document changes (see clause 4.5.2).

In some circumstances, it may be necessary to arrange for additional certification of new product systems.

If the development of a new or modified product, process, or application involves a contract agreement, the terms of this section of the Standard apply and a contract review (see clause 4.3) should be conducted.

This entire clause of the Standard is not covered in Q92 or Q93. If no contract agreements are involved in development activities, and no purchaser servicing (see clause 4.19) is conducted, Q92 should be considered for implementation.

Q91–1987 Standard

4.4.2 Design and Development Planning

The supplier shall draw up plans that identify the responsibility for each design and development activity. The plans shall describe or reference these activities and shall be updated as the design evolves.

GUIDANCE

Comprehensive planning for design activities includes research, development, scale-up, and introduction of a new product, application, service, or process. The plans referred to will be specific to each project. Plans specify the groups within the organization (and outside subcontractors) responsible for various aspects of the development, input data required for their work, resources they will require and results to be generated, stages at which project review will be held, and so on. It is understood that many aspects of a project will depend on results not available at the time of initial planning; this means that plans should be continually reviewed and updated during the course of the project so that nothing "falls through the cracks."

The supplier's plan should consider all elements specially addressed in the purchaser's contract (see clause 4.3):

- Purchaser requirements including product performance, quantity, package, possible purchaser process modifications

- Process engineering such as process condition and controls, pilot plant operation

- Engineering issues such as construction design and development

- Quality control including specifications for raw materials, intermediates and final products; measurement procedures and sampling plans

- Field evaluation may include conducting and evaluating application tests

- Safety issues should include review of process and product hazards

- Regulatory issues such as material safety data sheets, local requirements, prior notice of manufacture, registration and approval, and waste disposal procedures

- Documentation required by the contract

Q91–1987 Standard

4.4.2.1 Activity Assignment

The design and verification activities shall be planned and assigned to qualified staff equipped with adequate resources.

GUIDANCE

Personnel involved in a project should be qualified (see clause 4.18) by education, training, and/or experience. They should receive adequate time, funding, and support to carry out the tasks assigned.

Q91–1987 Standard

4.4.2.2 Organizational and Technical Interfaces

Organizational and technical interfaces between different groups shall be identified and the necessary information documented, transmitted, and regularly reviewed.

GUIDANCE

Good communication is essential for good development and design. The planning process should ensure that necessary information is documented and communicated among the groups involved, both internal and external. Interfacing is typically required among personnel in the areas of sales/marketing, research, engineering, quality assurance, purchasing, production, technical service, and regulatory, as well as subcontractors of equipment, raw materials, and services.

Q91–1987 Standard

4.4.3 Design Input

Design input requirements relating to the product shall be identified, documented, and their selection reviewed by the supplier for adequacy.

Incomplete, ambiguous, or conflicting requirements shall be resolved with those responsible for drawing up these requirements.

GUIDANCE

Project objectives should be adequately defined and clear to all involved.

In many CPI projects, a detailed and specific definition of design input requirements may not be possible in the early stages, since important characteristics of a material may be impossible to specify until the product is created or has demonstrated its performance in a prospective purchaser's application. Full-scale process development frequently begins only after the testing of prototypes, prepared in relatively small quantities, has created a market for the product.

Full specification of the product may even depend on data only available from testing of material from the scaled-up process. When this is the case, close cooperation between supplier and purchasers is especially vital, and ongoing communication of product requirements and process capability should be explicitly planned.

Q91–1987 Standard

4.4.4 Design Output

Design output shall be documented and expressed in terms of requirements, calculations, and analyses.

Design output shall:

    a) meet the design input requirements;

    b) contain or reference acceptance criteria;

    c) conform to appropriate regulatory requirements whether or not these have been stated in the input information;

    d) identify those characteristics of the design that are crucial to the safe and proper functioning of the product.

GUIDANCE

The documentation should not only define the specifications of the product and process but also describe in detail the reasoning behind the conception of the product, the design, and the operation of a process facility. Among the elements of documentation for a chemical product or process are:

- Product specifications

- Physical properties, material safety data sheets for products, packaging, and shelf-life

- Approved raw materials sources

- Sampling, procedures, and test methods

- Safety and environmental factors relevant to handling the product

Q91–1987 Standard

4.4.5 Design Verification

The supplier shall plan, establish, document, and assign to competent personnel functions for verifying the design.

Design verification shall establish that design output meets the design input requirement (see 4.4.4) by means of design control measures such as:

a) holding and recording design reviews (see 4.16);

b) undertaking qualification tests and demonstrations;

c) carrying out alternative calculations;

d) comparing the new design with a similar proven design, if available.

GUIDANCE

Development plans should include reviews at appropriate project stages. This may include review of data and calculations relating to plant designs for potential hazards of manufacture, readiness of distribution and field service functions, and so on.

At the conclusion of each phase of design or development a documented, systematic review of the design results should be conducted. Participants at each design review should include representatives of all functions affecting quality at the phase being reviewed. To assure objectivity, the design review should be conducted by personnel not involved in the design work being reviewed (see clause 4.1.2.2).

As appropriate to the design phase, verify the following:

• Items pertaining to purchaser needs and satisfaction

• Items pertaining to product specification and service requirements

• Items pertaining to process specifications and service requirements

Design verification may be undertaken independently or in support of design reviews by applying the following methods:

- Alternative calculations, made to verify the correctness of the original calculations and analyses

- Testing; e.g., by model or prototype tests—If this method is adopted, the test programs should be clearly defined and the results documented

- Independent verification, to verify the correctness of the original calculations and/or other design activities

The results of the final design review should be documented in specifications and drawings that define the design. The total document package defining the design should require approval of management affected by or contributing to the product. This approval constitutes the production release and authorizes that the design can be realized.

Q91–1987 Standard

4.4.6 Design Changes

The supplier shall establish and maintain procedures for the identi-fication, documentation, and appropriate review and approval of all changes and modifications.

GUIDANCE

Examples of design changes for which review and documentation requirements apply include changes to raw materials, product compo-sition or formulation, process conditions or procedures, testing proce-dures, specifications, packaging, and labels.

Design change procedures should define the company functions which are responsible for review and approval of a given change. Functions may include product management, quality assurance, engineering, development, research, legal, regulatory, and others as appropriate. Purchaser review of changes may also be appropriate because of the potential for unforeseen product performance effects.

Design change procedures should ensure compliance with document control procedures (see clause 4.5).

4.5 DOCUMENT CONTROL

INTRODUCTION: This clause of the Standard covers the requirement for maintaining, revising, and issuing those documents which can affect the quality of products or services. It is important that those who use the documents have the correct information.

Q91–1987 Standard

4.5 Document Control

4.5.1 Document Approval and Issue

The supplier shall establish and maintain procedures to control all documents and data that relate to the requirements of this Standard. These documents shall be reviewed and approved for adequacy by authorized personnel prior to issue. This control shall ensure that:

a) the pertinent issues of appropriate documents are available at all locations where operations essential to the effective functioning of the quality system are performed;

continued

---

continued

b) obsolete documents are promptly removed from all points of issue or use.

GUIDANCE

The Standard requires the supplier to control all documents that are within the scope of the quality system. To implement effective control of documents, the supplier should identify quality documents, data, and records. Procedures should define the mechanisms of control, including determining who needs the information and provisions for updating the information. The following are often classified as controlled documents:

- Quality manuals

- Policies

- Specifications (raw material, process, manufacturing, product, and package)

- Order entry procedures

- Training manuals and procedures

- Standard operating procedures

- Laboratory test methods

- Sampling plans

- Work instructions

The supplier should have the required documentation at the necessary locations. The documentation should provide concise instruction and should cover quality issues. In addition, documents should be:

- Properly reviewed and approved

- Dated, titled, and uniquely identified

- Distributed to locations for use

- Removed from service when changed or made obsolete

Q91-1987 Standard

4.5.2 Document Changes/Modifications

Changes to documents shall be reviewed and approved by the same functions/organizations that performed the original review and approval unless specifically designated otherwise. The designated organizations shall have access to pertinent background information upon which to base their review and approval.

Where practicable, the nature of the change shall be identified in the document or the appropriate attachments.

A master list or equivalent document control procedure shall be established to identify the current revision of documents in order to preclude the use of non-applicable documents.

Documents shall be re-issued after a practical number of changes have been made.

GUIDANCE

The supplier should ensure that only the most current version of a controlled document is available at the point of use. This process requires that the supplier know which is the appropriate or most current revision of a document. In larger organizations, or where document issuers and users are at different locations, it may be necessary to use some form of "acknowledgment of receipt" of amendments, revisions, or notices of change to ensure control.

A document control master list is one way to keep track of controlled documents within each function. Common items listed on a document control master list include functional responsibility, review/approval authority, document titles, current date and revision number, and the current holders of the document.

There should also be provisions for issuing controlled documents that will not be kept current (i.e., when issuing a quality manual to a purchaser). Controlled documents which are not kept current are often referred to as uncontrolled documents. The supplier should stamp "uncontrolled copy" on such documents.

Q91 clause 4.5, Document Control, is identical to clause 4.4 of Q92 and clause 4.3 of Q93.

4.6 PURCHASING

INTRODUCTION: This clause of the Standard deals with the purchasing requirements. The function of purchasing from sub-contractors should be planned and carried out under adequate control, including assessment and selection of sub-contractors, assurance of purchasing documents, and verification of purchased product. (For definitions of terms in this section, see the Introduction and also Figure 4.6-1 on page 35.)

Q91–1987 Standard

4.6.1 General

The supplier shall ensure that purchased product conforms to specified requirements.

GUIDANCE

Quality assurance for procuring materials and services includes systems to assure the following:

- Selection and qualification of sub-contractors capable of consistently meeting requirements (see clause 4.6.2)

- Clear and unambiguous definition and documentation of specifications and other requirements (see clause 4.6.3)

Establishing effective procedures for control of the quality of purchased product should include activities designed to prevent non-conformances.

Q91–1987 Standard

4.6.2 Assessment of Sub-Contractors

The supplier shall select sub-contractors on the basis of their ability to meet sub-contract requirements, including quality requirements. The supplier shall establish and maintain records of acceptable sub-contractors (see 4.16).

The selection of sub-contractors, and the type and extent of control exercised by the supplier, shall be dependent upon the type of product and, where appropriate, on records of sub-contractors' previously demonstrated capability and performance.

The supplier shall ensure that quality system controls are effective.

GUIDANCE

Sub-contractors should be selected for their ability to consistently meet product and service requirements at a total cost that provides the best value.

Assessment of the sub-contractor's ability to consistently meet requirements may be based on evidence such as:

- On-site assessment and evaluation of the sub-contractor's capability and quality system by the supplier

- Reviews and assessment of sub-contractors' and/or suppliers' quality and/or performance data

- Trials or demonstrations in the supplier's laboratories or plant

- Documented evidence of successful use in similar processes

- Third party assessments and registration of the sub-contractor's quality systems to an accepted Standard such as Q91 or Q92

The assessment method selected should ensure that purchased product consistently meets requirements.

The supplier should maintain assessment data and records of acceptable sub-contractors. ("Approved" is a term commonly used in the CPI for an acceptable sub-contractor.) There should be periodic reviews of the sub-contractor's acceptability, performed at intervals consistent with the complexity and technical requirements of the product.

The supplier is permitted to determine what constitutes evidence of an acceptable quality system. Assessment against an appropriate standard such as Q91 may be used to provide the evidence.

"Purchase for resale" (PFR) product when sold should meet all the clauses of the Standard as would all the other parts of supplier business.

Current and historical data may be used to assess the sub-contractor's capability to meet requirements consistently. Statistical evaluation of the data should demonstrate that the sub-contractor's process has been maintained in a state of control and that it is capable of meeting specified requirements (see clause 4.20).

Q91–1987 Standard

4.6.3 Purchasing Data

Purchasing documents shall contain data clearly describing the product ordered, including, where applicable:

a) the type, class, style, grade, or other precise identification;

b) the title or other positive identification, and applicable issue of specifications, drawings, process requirements, inspection instructions, and other relevant technical data, including requirements for approval or qualification of product, procedures, process equipment and personnel;

continued

---

continued

   c) the title, number, and issue of the quality system Standard to be
      applied to the product.

The supplier shall review and approve purchasing documents for
adequacy of specified requirements prior to release.

GUIDANCE

In the chemical or process industry, purchasing data are usually
communicated to the sub-contractor through a contract or purchase
order with attendant specifications. Quality requirements are generally
contained in a detailed specification. Individual shipments under a
purchase order are often covered by a *release* which refers to the
requirements of the original purchase order rather than repeating them.

Detailed specifications contain the complete requirements of the
supplier. These include, for example:

- Chemical composition with target values and limits

- Physical form and composition with size distribution values and
  limits

- Performance characteristics with values and limits

- Sampling, inspection, and test methods

- Packaging, labeling, and transportation

Quality assurance requirements are usually considered part of the
detailed specification:

- The quality system standard under which the product shall be
  produced

- Quality system and manufacturing process change notification

- Regulatory requirements (e.g., FDA, EPA, DoD, etc.)

The purchase order or contract should specify:

- Quantity and price

- Delivery date and location

- Product quality data required for this shipment, e.g., quality certificate, control charts

- Delivery of product quality data

- Pre-shipment sample requirement

- Point of ownership transfer

The supplier's purchasing data and documents should be reviewed for accuracy and completeness and approved by authorized personnel before release.

Conferences with sub-contractors will help ensure that requirements are clearly defined and understood. The sub-contractor should review the purchase documents and acknowledge acceptance of all requirements specified in the purchase documents. Acceptance should become a part of the supplier's quality records.

Q91–1987 Standard

4.6.4 Verification of Purchased Product

Where specified in the contract, the purchaser or the purchaser's representative shall be afforded the right to verify at source or upon receipt that purchased product conforms to specified requirements. Verification by the purchaser shall not absolve the supplier of the responsibility to provide subsequent rejection.

When the purchaser or the purchaser's representative elects to carry out verification at the sub-contractor's plant, such verification shall not be used by the supplier as evidence of effective control of quality by the sub-contractor.

GUIDANCE

In CPI, the purchaser generally does not have specifications on raw materials used by the supplier to manufacture products. Thus, quality conformation of raw materials purchased by the supplier may not be subject to verification by the purchaser. The verification stops at the review of raw material specification approval, incoming inspection, and material approval unless specifically addressed in the contract.

When the material or item purchased from the sub-contractor remains unchanged (i.e., a single material produced for direct sale or an item incorporated into a product in an unchanged condition) and the product formulation is specified by the purchaser, then verification by the purchaser of the sub-contractor is a valid request.

If the purchaser has a special need for verification by the sub-contractor to assure that the product or service conforms to specified requirements, the contract between the supplier and the purchaser or sub-contractor should include special clauses or statements that such verification is required (see Figure 4.6-2 on page 35).

When specified in the contract, the purchaser may extend verification activities to the sub-contractor's facilities to assure that the product conforms to specified requirements. A variation of verification at source is a pre-shipment sample contract (which holds inventory for shipment for a specified time until the purchaser verifies). In such cases, the supplier may arrange for the purchaser to assess the quality of the sub-contractor's product and/or the effectiveness of the process. Where the contract provides, the purchaser may use the supplier's data to decide which of the products will require verification at source and to decide the nature and extent of such verification.

The supplier is responsible for assuring that purchased product conforms to all specifications and requirements of the contract. The purchaser's verification at sub-contractor does not absolve the supplier of responsibility, nor does it preclude subsequent rejection.

There are special supplier–purchaser situations that could require verification at sub-contractor plant, such as purchase through a chemical distributor or reseller. In this case, the distributor is the supplier, but the contract could require verification from the manufacturer (the sub-contractor). A similar case would be a product exchange arranged by a third party.

Q91 clause 4.6 is identical to clause 4.5 of Q92 and is not covered in Q93.

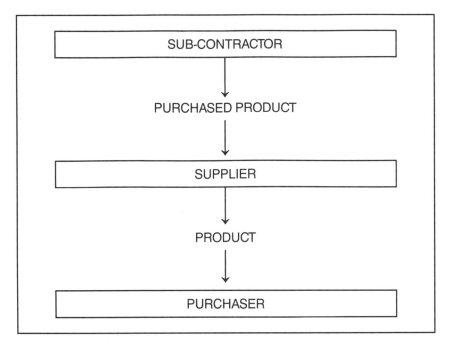

Figure 4.6-1   Relationships of Sub-Contractor, Supplier, and Purchaser

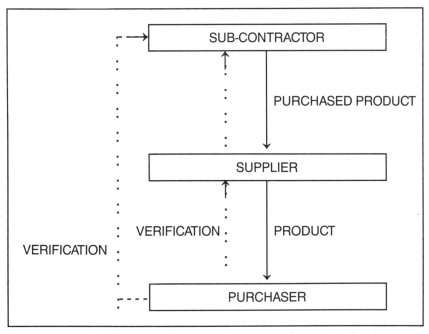

Figure 4.6-2   Verification of Purchased Product at Source by Purchaser

4.7 PURCHASER SUPPLIED PRODUCT

INTRODUCTION: This clause of the Standard covers requirements for control of product supplied by the purchaser.

Q91–1987 Standard

4.7 Purchaser Supplied Product

The supplier shall establish and maintain procedures for verification, storage, and maintenance of purchaser supplied product provided for incorporation into the supplies. Any such product that is lost, damaged, or is otherwise unsuitable for use shall be recorded and reported to the purchaser (see 4.16).

NOTE: Verification by the supplier does not absolve the purchaser of the responsibility to provide acceptable product.

GUIDANCE

Purchaser supplied product is product owned by the purchaser and furnished to the supplier for use in meeting the requirements of the contract (see Figure 4.7-1 on page 39). The supplier will need to install control systems to assure material and quality accountability for products supplied by the purchaser.

Purchaser supplied product may be either materials or services. In the process industry, materials may include raw materials, additives, blend components, containers, or packaging material. Services may include testing, inspections, transportation, or packaging.

This clause also applies to conversion or toll manufacturing arrangements between the purchaser and supplier where the purchaser provides materials or services.

Consideration should be given to the following:

- Purchaser is responsible for providing acceptable materials or services

- Supplier should verify the quantities, quality, and condition of purchaser supplied product on receipt

- Supplier accepts responsibility for maintaining traceability and accountability of the material until returned under the terms of the agreement or contract

The supplier should establish and use quality assurance procedures which conform to the requirements of Q91 for purchaser supplied product unless special procedures are specified in the contract with the purchaser (see clause 4.10.1). These procedures will include maintaining records and reporting to the purchaser any purchaser supplied product that is lost, damaged, or otherwise unsuitable for use.

The requirements of clause 4.16, Quality Records, should be met for purchaser supplied materials.

Q91 clause 4.7 is identical to clause 4.6 of Q92 and is not covered in Q93.

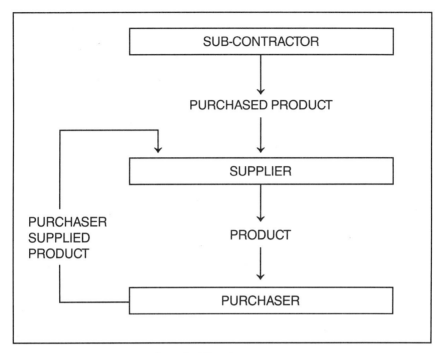

Figure 4.7-1 Purchaser Supplied Product

4.8 PRODUCT IDENTIFICATION AND TRACEABILITY

INTRODUCTION: This clause of the Standard covers requirements for identification and traceability of product.

Q91-1987 Standard

4.8 Product Identification and Traceability

Where appropriate, the supplier shall establish and maintain procedures for identifying the product from applicable drawings, specifications, or other documents, during all stages of production, delivery, and installation.

Where, and to the extent that, traceability is a specified requirement, individual product or batches shall have a unique identification. This identification shall be recorded (see 4.16).

GUIDANCE

Product *identification* provides the means of distinguishing one product from another. This includes similar products, such as those constituting a product line, as well as like products manufactured at different times or locations. Identification ensures that production personnel can determine which of several similar products or grades of product they are working on.

Product *traceability* provides a record of one product unit's manufacturing history, including the identification of raw materials and intermediates used in its production. A fundamental requisite to either function is a working definition of what constitutes a batch or lot for raw materials, intermediates, and finished products. Traceability provides a means of tracking product so that if a nonconformity or other problem is discovered after the product has passed final inspection and testing, all affected purchasers can be promptly notified. Traceability also facilitates cause and effect analysis, making it easier to understand the process and make corrections and improvements. For example, this can be helpful if a process shift can be traced to a change in raw materials.

It is often difficult to designate or identify precise lots or batches from a continuous process. Even in the case of a batch process, the batch identity is often difficult to maintain due to downstream blending. Identification and traceability of some bulk products may only be accomplished through recording of times, flow rates, and location; use of tags or other discrete identifiers may be inappropriate or impossible.

Product identification should be addressed in the following manner:

- The product identification system should be documented and maintained.

- Each product should be uniquely identifiable during the manufacturing, storage, delivery, and installation process.

- Each product should be identified and have applicable product and manufacturing specifications, drawings, and/or technical data sheets which provide sufficient information to distinguish one product from another.

- Unique product identification should be an integral part of the manufacturing (see clauses 4.9, 4.12, and 4.13) and the handling, packing, storage, and delivery operations (see clause 4.15).

Product traceability should be addressed in the following manner:

- The product traceability system should be documented and maintained.

- Batches or lots should have unique identification codes.

- Product traceability records should be retained in accordance with the quality records (see clause 4.16) requirements.

- Product traceability data may include batch numbers of raw materials, production and laboratory data generated during manufacturing process, records of product disposition, and applicable purchaser information, although the Standard does not require this.

- Traceability should be possible both from the raw materials to the finished product, and from the finished product back to the raw materials.

Clause 4.8 of Q91 is identical to clause 4.7 in Q92. Q93 only refers to product identification where it is contractually specified (see clause 4.4). It does not address traceability.

4.9 PROCESS CONTROL

INTRODUCTION: This clause of the Standard defines the requirements for a system to manage and control production operations that affect quality. The objective is to achieve consistent, predictable production operations in conformance with requirements.

In the CPI, the term *process control* usually refers to a system (often computerized) of sensors, and analyzers and controllers with feedback loops. However, the Standard uses the term in a broader sense to encompass all of the production operations. It does not cover packaging and distribution (see clause 4.15) unless these are the principal production operations.

Q91–1987 Standard

4.9.1 General

The supplier shall identify and plan the production and, where applicable, installation processes which directly affect quality and shall ensure that these processes are carried out under controlled conditions. Controlled conditions shall include the following:

continued

---

continued

a) documented work instructions defining the manner of production and installation, where the absence of such instruction would adversely affect quality, use of suitable production and installation equipment, suitable working environment, compliance with reference standards/codes, and quality plans;

b) monitoring and control of suitable process and product characteristics during production and installation;

c) the approval of processes and equipment, as appropriate;

d) criteria for workmanship which shall be stipulated, to the greatest practicable extent, in written standards or by means of representative samples.

GUIDANCE

Establishing an effective process control system requires knowledge of the process and of the relationship between product characteristics and the key process variables. Process knowledge and determination of these relationships begin in research (see clause 4.4). Learning continues throughout the life of the product life cycle (see clauses 4.10, 4.13, and 4.16).

The process control system should provide:

a) Operator work instructions (process recipe, work order, batch sheet, or write-ups) which specify:

- Safety requirements

- The operation in terms understandable to the reader

- What to do should a process upset occur

- Raw material quality requirements

- Equipment and preventive maintenance requirements

- The steps to be followed to carry out the operation

- Specify sampling requirements

- Environmental requirements needed to preserve product quality

- Values and/or limit requirements for process variables

- Values and/or limit requirements for product characteristics

- The handling requirements needed to preserve product quality

- The process variable and product measurements required

- Whom to contact concerning changes to the operation

b) Control strategies for each of the key process variables and key product characteristics, which:

  - Should specify the actions to be taken to keep key process variables and product characteristics within requirements

  - Require accurate measurement data

  - Indicate where control of variability is necessary

  - Describe appropriate statistical tools

    Clauses 4.10.1, 4.10.2, 4.11, and 4.20 apply to production control.

c) A process for approving operator work instructions and operations equipment to ensure that instructions and equipment are correct and capable. Approval is needed when the operation or equipment is new or has been changed.

d) Criteria for workmanship that allows operating personnel to make decisions concerning the acceptability of their work. In CPI, the appearance of a product is often the only aspect that an operator can judge firsthand. Verification of product quality by analytical means often takes time because of the location of analytical tools and the time to obtain results. Thus, clear descriptions and/or samples of acceptable and unacceptable appearance should always be provided to the operators. Criteria can be expressed in words and by examples. The criteria should clearly describe both acceptable and unacceptable product where possible.

Physical descriptions of appearance such as:

- Fine brown powder free of foreign contaminants

- Green clear liquid

- Milk white uniform emulsion

- Uniform free flowing mixture of green and tan spheres

Examples such as:

- Finished packages

- Damaged or deformed product

- Contaminated product

- Labeling

- Color standards, etc.

Q91–1987 Standard

4.9.2 Special Processes

These are processes, the results of which cannot be fully verified by subsequent inspection and testing of the product and where, for example, processing deficiencies may become apparent only after the product is in use. Accordingly, continuous monitoring and/or compliance with documented procedures is required to ensure that the specified requirements are met. These processes shall be qualified and shall also comply with the requirements of 4.9.1.

Records shall be maintained for qualified processes, equipment, and personnel, as appropriate.

GUIDANCE

CPI processes are generally considered special processes. Process records should be kept. There should be a system for qualification of quality sensitive equipment, process, operators, and technicians wherever quality may be impacted. Verification of special processes should address:

- The accuracy and variability of equipment used to make or measure product, including settings and adjustments

- Skill, capability, and knowledge of operators to meet quality requirements

- Special environments, time, temperature, or other factors affecting quality

- Maintenance of qualification records for personnel, processes, and equipment, as appropriate

- Frequency of verification, based on a study of the stability of the process in which process limits are defined

This clause of Q91 is identical to clause 4.8 in Q92 and is not covered in Q93.

4.10 INSPECTION AND TESTING

INTRODUCTION: This clause of the Standard covers requirements for inspection and testing of incoming products, in-process materials, and final products. It applies to laboratory, on-line, and process measurements.

Sampling plans are essential elements of inspection and testing. These plans should consider:

- Sampling methodology

- Whether or not the test is destructive

- Process capability

- Test capability

- Sample stability

- Measurement error in proportion to total variability

- Time to complete test relative to process cycle times

- Time for process to stabilize following an upset or intentional change

- Purchaser or statutory requirements

- Cost of failure to detect a nonconformance

- Cost of test

- Uniformity of sample

- Ability of sample to truly represent the product

Q91–1987 Standard

4.10.1 Receiving Inspection and Testing

4.10.1.1 The supplier shall ensure that product is not used or processed (except in the circumstances described in 4.10.1.2) until it has been inspected or otherwise verified as conforming to specified requirements. Verification shall be in accordance with the quality plan or documented procedures.

GUIDANCE

This clause applies to *purchased products* (see clause 4.6) and *purchaser supplied products* (see clause 4.7). Receiving inspection includes verifying that sub-contractors have fulfilled their contractual obligations for quality and that procured items or substances entering suppliers' facilities meet specified requirements. This verification applies to service and product aspects of incoming material.

Positive identification and traceability of purchased materials through the process is not a strict requirement but is strongly recommended. It will significantly ease investigations regarding corrective action (see clause 4.14) and will permit compliance with any requirements regarding traceability (see clause 4.8). A related area is requirements for inspection and test status (see clause 4.12).

The method used to ensure quality of purchased materials and services received by the supplier depends on the importance of the item to product or process quality, the state of control (process or product), past performance of the sub-contractor, information available from the sub-contractor, and impact on costs (see clauses 9.7 and 9.8 of Q94).

Both bulk and packaged materials should be segregated to avoid consumption before acceptance. The supplier should maintain sufficient control and traceability, even if pipeline shipments or large tanks are involved.

Introduction of new bulk materials into the inventory of existing materials raises the potential for cross-contamination. In some cases (e.g., pipeline shipments), raw materials proceed directly from the sub-contractor's process without going into inventory and are immediately consumed in the supplier's process. Such cases require a high level of confidence in the sub-contractor's quality system.

This element does not imply that incoming items must be inspected and tested by the supplier; however, safety concerns dictate positive identification. Receiving verification of other specifications can be limited to checking objective evidence provided by sub-contractors. The basis for verification method should be documented (e.g., certificates of analysis).

The supplier's procedures for receiving inspection should include the means of verifying that shipments are complete, properly identified, undamaged, and accompanied by supporting documentation if required (e.g., test reports or control charts).

Procedures should also specify corrective actions to follow in the event of nonconformance (see clause 4.14). Analysis of past receiving inspection data can influence the supplier's decisions regarding the need to reassess the sub-contractor's capabilities (see clause 4.20).

Q91–1987 Standard

4.10.1.2 Where incoming product is released for urgent production purposes, it shall be positively identified and recorded (see 4.16) in order to permit immediate recall and replacement in the event of noncon-formance to specified requirements.

GUIDANCE

This clause of the Standard covers the situation in which material is used before verification is complete. In this case, the Standard REQUIRES total traceability.

Acceptance and use of incoming product subject to recall should be STRONGLY DISCOURAGED as a matter of good quality management practice. Items should be released only if:

- An objective evaluation of quality status and resolution on any nonconformity can still be implemented

- Correction of nonconformity cannot compromise the quality of adjacent, attached, or incorporated items

To achieve the control required, avoid acceptance of bulk raw materials without appropriate receiving inspection. Once product has been pumped into tanks or blown into silos, its positive identification may be lost through mixing with existing inventory. For package products, the sub-contractor's batch numbers may provide adequate positive identification.

Q91–1987 Standard

4.10.1 Receiving, Inspection and Testing (Note)

NOTE: In determining the amount and nature of receiving inspection, consideration should be given to the control exercised at source and documented evidence of quality conformance provided.

GUIDANCE

Incoming product acceptance procedures should be developed, taking into consideration process requirements and sub-contractor's process capability (see clause 4.20). The goal is to minimize or eliminate the need for formal incoming lot acceptance and to rely on the sub-contractor to supply product that continually meet requirements. Supporting documentation may be required in the form of certification, data sharing, or statistical evidence. Minimal inspection or testing may still be required for identification, to detect changes that occur during shipment or for safety reasons.

Q91–1987 Standard

4.10.2 In-Process Inspection and Testing

The supplier shall:

a) inspect, test, and identify product as required by the quality plan or documented procedures;

b) establish product conformance to specified requirements by use of process monitoring and control methods;

c) hold product until the required inspection and tests have been completed or necessary reports have been received and verified except when product is released under positive recall procedures (see 4.10.1). Release under positive recall procedures shall not preclude the activities outlined in 4.10.2 a);

d) identify nonconforming product.

GUIDANCE

In-process inspection and testing applies to all forms of products, including services. This includes all tests performed after incoming inspection and before final inspection. These test results are often used both to control the process and to verify conformance to requirements.

Measurements that are critical to quality must be identified and controlled as part of the quality management system. This includes documented action plans in the event of failure of critical instruments.

Inspections or tests should be considered at appropriate points in the process to verify conformity. Location and frequency will depend on the importance of the characteristics and ease of verification at the stage of production.

Verification should be made as close as possible to the point where the feature or characteristic is first measurable.

Many process industries are heavily dependent upon on-line analyzers and instruments to control important process parameters to target values and/or within approved ranges.

In-process inspection and testing may include:

• Sensors used by automatic controllers or by operators for feed-back/feedforward loops (e.g., flow control)

- Automatic analysis or inspection (e.g., material composition by on-line gas chromatographs and infrared scanners)

- Off-line chemical and physical analyses (e.g., composition of sample)

- Instrument observations by process operators (e.g. temperature readings)

- Designated physical inspection stations within the process (e.g., visual inspection of color)

Statistical process control methodology will often provide early warning of problems before nonconformities occur.

The points of control and the acceptable ranges should be defined for each of the in-process measurements. In general, product should be held until required verification have been completed. Nonconforming product needs to be identified and controlled (see clause 4.13).

Documented work instructions (see clause 4.9.1) should indicate the corrective actions to be followed when values for monitored parameter fall outside the acceptable range (see clause 4.13).

Q91–1987 Standard

4.10.3 Final Inspection and Testing

The quality plan or documented procedures for final inspection and testing shall require that all specified inspection and tests, including those specified either on receipt of product or in-process, have been carried out and that the data meets specified requirements.

The supplier shall carry out all final inspection and testing in accordance with the quality plan or documented procedures to complete the evidence of conformance of the finished product to the specified requirements.

No product shall be dispatched until all activities specified in the quality plan or documented procedures have been satisfactorily completed and the associated data and documentation is available and authorized.

GUIDANCE

The requirements of this section apply to finished product and service before shipment. This is the point in the quality assurance system where the supplier generates evidence that the finished product meets specified requirements.

Final inspection is defined as the activities (examination, inspection, measurement, or test) upon which the release of product or service with respect to specified characteristics is based. Suitable procedures should be established so that each unit or lot of product or service is not released until the required inspections and tests show that the product or service meets specified requirements.

Finished product verification has these important roles:

- To confirm predictions based on process parameters

- To guide longer term process adjustments

- To provide the basis for product acceptance or rejection

- To provide data for statistical analysis of process and product performance

To augment inspections and tests made during production, two forms of final verification of finished product are available. Either of the following may be used, as appropriate:

- Final inspections or tests to ensure that items or lots produced have met performance and other quality requirements. Reference should be made to the purchase order to verify that product to be shipped agrees in type and quantity. Examples include 100 percent inspection, lot sampling, and continuous sampling. In the case of product released via pipeline, consider use of on-line analyzers.

- Prediction of conformance based on process knowledge and test results.

Release inspection and product quality auditing may provide feedback for corrective action on product and process.

Q91–1987 Standard

4.10.4 Inspection and Test Records

The supplier shall establish and maintain records which give evidence that the product has passed inspection and/or test with defined acceptance criteria (see 4.16).

GUIDANCE

Records are needed to show that the required inspections have been made on the purchased product properties, the specified in-process parameters, and the final product (see clause 4.16).

In circumstances where in-process training inspection and testing are achieved by monitoring in-process instrumental control, the records for this part of the inspection should also be kept (see clause 4.16).

If certificates of analysis were used during receiving inspection procedures, then these certificates will form part of the inspection and test records.

Inspection and test records should be easily accessible.

This clause in Q91 is clause 4.9 in Q92 and clause 4.5 in Q93.

4.11 INSPECTION, MEASURING, AND TEST EQUIPMENT

INTRODUCTION: This clause of the Standard covers requirements for inspection, measuring, and test equipment. It applies to equipment used in meeting the requirements for receiving, in-process, and final inspection and testing (see clauses 4.10.1, 4.10.2, and 4.10.3). It is helpful to approach this element from the perspective that each measurement system is a process involving materials, equipment, procedures, and people.

Q91–1987 Standard

4.11 Inspection, Measuring, and Test Equipment

The supplier shall control, calibrate, and maintain inspection, measuring, and test equipment, whether owned by the supplier, on loan, or provided by the purchaser, to demonstrate the conformance of product to the specified requirements. Equipment shall be used in a manner which ensures that measurement uncertainty is known and is consistent with the required measurement capability.

GUIDANCE

Sufficient control should be maintained over all measurement systems used in the development, manufacture, installation, and servicing of a product to provide confidence in any decisions or actions based on measurement data. Control should be exercised over gages, instruments, sensors, special test equipment, and related computer software. In addition, process instrumentation that can affect the specified characteristics of a product or service should be suitably controlled (see clause 11.3 of Q94).

For both product and service measurement systems, statistical methods are valuable tools for achieving and demonstrating conformity to requirements. In particular, statistical methods are preferred tools in fulfilling the overall requirement that "equipment shall be used in a manner which ensures that measurement uncertainty is known and is consistent with the required measurement capability." These methods may also be used to monitor and maintain critical measurement systems in a state of statistical control (see clause 4.20).

The following subparts spell out in detail what is to be implemented in the measurement quality assurance system.

Q91–1987 Standard

4.11 Inspection, Measuring and Test Equipment

The supplier shall:

a) identify the measurements to be made, the accuracy required, and select the appropriate inspection, measuring, and test equipment;

GUIDANCE

The supplier will need to identify all measurements required to demonstrate that the product is in conformance with requirements (see clause 4.10). This will include measurements of purchased product, process control measurements, and measurements of the finished product or service. In general terms, wherever inspection, measuring, or test equipment provides data required by the quality system, then the equipment should be identified, controlled, calibrated, and maintained in accordance with the requirements of clause 4.11.

The equipment referred to here is restricted to that used to control and/or verify product quality. Plant instrumentation and test equipment provided for purposes such as safety, environmental control, or energy or material usages, may remain outside the quality system. However, consider including *all* critical inspection, test, or measurement equipment in the quality assurance system for measurements, regardless of purpose.

For each measurement, test equipment must be specified and selected that will provide the appropriate precision, accuracy, robustness, and reliability under actual conditions of service.

Q91–1987 Standard

4.11 Inspection, Measuring, and Test Equipment

The supplier shall:

b) identify, calibrate, and adjust all inspection, measuring and test equipment, and devices that can affect product quality at pre-scribed intervals, or prior to use, against certified equipment having a known valid relationship to nationally recognized standards — where no such standards exist, the basis used for calibration shall be documented;

GUIDANCE

The calibration of inspection, measuring, and test equipment should include the following:

- Initial checking of calibration prior to use, verifying conformance to the required accuracy and precision. The software and procedures controlling automatic test equipment should also be verified.

- Periodic scheduled checks of the measurement systems. When outside of acceptance criteria, recalibration, adjustment, or repair must re-establish the required precision and accuracy in use. Recalibration should generally be done only when checks indicate the measurement system is statistically out of control. Excessive recalibration can increase total variability.

- Traceability of calibrants to national or international standards, if they exist. Where such recognized reference standards do not exist, internal standards may be used. Preparation and testing of these internal standards should be in accord with documented and approved procedures.

Guidance on the general requirements for assuring the quality of calibration may be found in the *ANSI/ASQC Standard M1–1987—Calibration Systems.*

The process industry frequently uses internal reference materials, together with statistical methods, to validate the complete measurement process. The use of a primary reference material or calibrant to check accuracy (lack of bias) often validates only part of a given measurement process.

Q91–1987 Standard

4.11 Inspection, Measuring, and Test Equipment

The supplier shall:

  c) establish, document, and maintain calibrating procedures, including details of equipment type, identification number, location, frequency of checks, check method, acceptance criteria, and the action to be taken when results are unsatisfactory;

GUIDANCE

The supplier should consider the following guidance in developing and documenting procedures:

- Calibration procedures must be documented, approved, maintained, and controlled as a part of the quality system. These procedures must define the acceptance criteria or limits and the frequency of checks.

- The acceptance criteria should be the precision and accuracy required for the most stringent of tests for which that equipment is used.

- The time interval between calibration checks and maintenance must be reasonable for the requirement; the supplier determines this based on experience and knowledge of how the equipment is used. The equipment and, where appropriate, materials used in testing must be checked, calibrated, and maintained according to written procedures.

- Where a measurement system is determined to be out of control or outside acceptance limits, corrective action is necessary. Review of statistical control records is often a necessary and useful step in identifying when and if corrective actions are needed. If statistical records show the measurement process to be out of control (i.e., a special cause exists), the user should remove the cause prior to recalibration.

Q91–1987 Standard

4.11 Inspection, Measuring, and Test Equipment

The supplier shall:

d) ensure that the inspection, measuring, and test equipment is capable of the accuracy and precision necessary;

GUIDANCE

Manufacturers of standard measuring gages or instruments will specify and, often, supply certification of the precision and accuracy of their equipment as shipped. These specifications or certifications of capability should be compared to the requirements of the process, contract, quality system, or test methods. Verification of the device's capability against the manufacturer's certification or specification is recommended. This information should be included in the documentation of the quality system for inspection, measuring, and test equipment.

In the process industry, complex measuring equipment and procedures are common. Development of special measurement systems should include determinations of precision and accuracy. Consider including the purchaser's laboratory in studies of test methods for finished products. These studies should be conducted using accepted procedures such as ASTM E691–87 *Standard Practice for Conducting an Interlaboratory Test Program to Determine the Precision of Test Methods.*

Evaluation of any measurement system's capability should include studies of the variation due to sampling. In the CPI, variance due to the sampling procedures is often highly significant. Control of sampling procedures is a necessary part of measurement system control.

Where computer software is used as part of the measurement system, it is necessary to test the performance of the software before it is used to release material for use or sale.

Q91–1987 Standard

4.11 Inspection, Measuring, and Test Equipment

The supplier shall:

  e) identify inspection, measuring, and test equipment with a suitable indicator or approved identification record to show the calibration status;

  f) maintain calibration records for inspection, measuring, and test equipment (see 4.16);

GUIDANCE

A widely used method for compliance with clause 4.11 subpart (e) is the physical tagging of each and every piece of inspection, measuring, or test equipment. The tag is marked with device identification, the current status of its calibration, the identification of the person who performed the calibration, and the next calibration date.

In the CPI, where hundreds of measuring devices are used in a production process, practical alternatives may be used, such as computer-based records with provisions for verification of calibration status. The user must be able to demonstrate that the system effectively prevents the use of measurements from a critical inspection, measuring, or test device when its calibration check is overdue.

In addition to the calibration status, records for each piece of inspection, measuring, or test equipment should include all of the data required in clause 4.11 subpart (c).

Routine maintenance and verification of the measurement system's precision and accuracy during production should include control charting of data obtained using references and/or standard samples.

For each measurement system included in the scope of this requirement, it is necessary to identify both equipment and materials used to make the measurements. The particular materials (e.g., standard analytical solutions and buffer solutions) should be identified by a tag number, label, or other suitable means which meets safety requirements and indicates the expiration date of the material.

Q91–1987 Standard

4.11 Inspection, Measuring, and Test Equipment

The supplier shall:

g) assess and document the validity of previous inspection and test results when inspection, measuring, and test equipment is found to be out of calibration;

GUIDANCE

When a measurement system is found to be out of calibration or out of statistical control, this subpart requires an assessment of previous measurements obtained with the measurement system. Product produced while measurements were in error may require retesting to verify conformance to requirements. Records must be maintained of the results of measurement verification, including any replacement of incorrect measurements in quality system records.

Q91–1987 Standard

4.11 Inspection, Measuring, and Test Equipment

The supplier shall:

h) ensure that the environmental conditions are suitable for the calibration, inspections, measurements, and test being carried out;

i) ensure that the handling, preservation, and storage of inspection, measuring, and test equipment is such that the accuracy and fitness for use is maintained;

j) safeguard inspection, measuring, and test facilities, including both test hardware and test software, from adjustments which would invalidate the calibration setting.

GUIDANCE

This section of the Standard contains requirements for ensuring that the capability of all inspection, measuring, and test equipment is protected from damage or inadvertent mis-adjustments. Appropriate protective devices, shielding, and work instructions should be incorporated into the quality system to protect this equipment. The environmental conditions appropriate for the measurement system should be continuously maintained.

Q91–1987 Standard

4.11 Inspection, Measuring, and Test Equipment (continued)

Where test hardware (e.g., jigs, fixtures, templates, patterns) or test software is used as suitable forms of inspection, they shall be checked to prove that they are capable of verifying the acceptability of product prior to release for use during production and installation and shall be re-checked at prescribed intervals. The supplier shall establish the extent and frequency of such checks and shall maintain records as evidence of control (see 4.16). Measurement design data shall be made available, when required by the purchaser or his representative, for verification that it is functionally adequate.

GUIDANCE

The requirement relating to test hardware or software will apply to such things as:

- Molds or dies used to prepare samples for testing

- Standard color plaques

- Reference samples used to evaluate appearance, fragrance, and other factors

- Test system software used for spectrum analysis, etc.

- Automatic titrators and gas chromatographic equipment

Records and data from measurement system design, development, and control should be kept. The purchaser or purchaser's representative may request and review this data to verify the adequacy of the supplier's measurement systems.

The requirements of this clause of Q91 are identical to clause 4.10 of Q92. The subject is mentioned in clause 4.6 of Q93 but does not include the detail of Q91 and Q92.

4.12 INSPECTION AND TEST STATUS

INTRODUCTION: This clause of the Standard augments requirements for product identification and traceability (see clause 4.8). It refers specifically to results of inspections and tests required by the quality system to know the status of product in process until the time of shipment.

Q91–1987 Standard

4.12 Inspection and Test Status

The inspection and test status of product shall be identified by using markings, authorized stamps, tags, labels, routing cards, inspection records, test software, physical location, or other suitable means, which indicate the conformance or nonconformance of product with regard to inspection and tests performed. The identification of inspection and test status shall be maintained, as necessary, throughout production and installation of the product to ensure that only product that has

continued

---

continued

passed the required inspections and tests is dispatched, used, or installed.

Records shall identify the inspection authority responsible for the release of conforming product (see 4.16).

GUIDANCE

The requirements apply to status of purchased products, isolated intermediates, and finished product.

Status of any material in storage or in-process, with respect to any test required by the quality system, should be available.

Test status of material is either: not yet tested, awaiting results, "passed," or "failed" (nonconforming).

Using stamps or tags for direct labeling of material's test status is often unsuitable for chemical products (see clause 4.8). Records of test results from the control laboratory, production logs, documentation of bulk shipments, or in a material control system (electronic or otherwise) are acceptable, but only if it is impossible to release or use a failed lot under the system. The supplier must demonstrate that the system provides adequate control.

The system should include positive controls which ensure that all required tests are performed and appropriate action taken on the results.

Separate storage areas for quarantine of uninspected or nonconforming material, or hold or day tanks for material awaiting testing, are sometimes employed. When material is not held, as in the case of a process feeding directly into a pipeline or further process, on-line controls that ensure conformance of material may be used.

Responsibility for release of conforming product must be assigned and documented (see clause 4.5). Retention of inspection and test records must be documented and maintained (see clause 4.16). For nonconforming product requirements, see clause 4.13.

Figure 4.12-1 on page 71 shows key decision steps.

This clause of Q91 has the same wording as clause 4.11 in Q92 and similar wording as clause 4.7 in Q93.

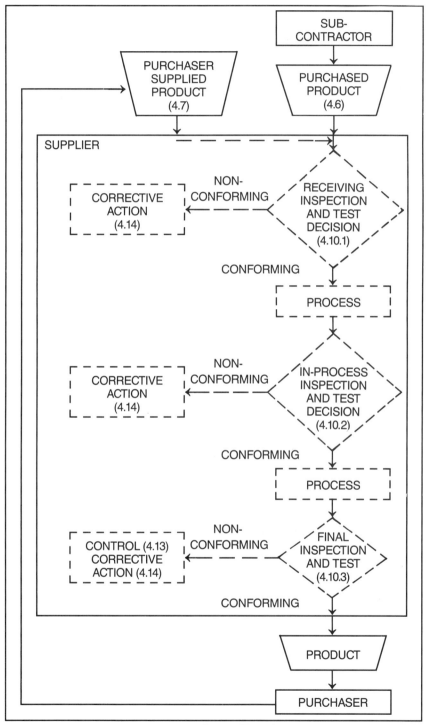

Figure 4.12-1 Inspection and Test Status Flowchart

4.13 CONTROL OF NONCONFORMING PRODUCT

INTRODUCTION: This clause of the Standard requires procedures to prevent the inadvertent use or dispatch of product that does not conform to specifications or requirements. It also addresses review and distribution of nonconforming product.

Q91–1987 Standard

4.13 Control of Nonconforming Product

The supplier shall establish and maintain procedures to ensure that product does not conform to specified requirements is prevented from inadvertent use or installation. Control shall provide for identification, documentation, evaluation, segregation when practical, disposition of nonconforming product, and for notification to the functions concerned.

GUIDANCE

Control systems need to be established which provide for identification, evaluation, segregation where practical, disposition and documentation of nonconforming product, and for notification of other functions that may be affected, including, where appropriate, the purchaser.

The positive system MUST prevent the inadvertent use or shipment of nonconforming or uninspected product. Wherever practical, nonconforming or uninspected product should be physically segregated from conforming product and clearly identified by marking or tagging.

In the process industry, certain handling methods such as pipeline distribution may prevent segregation of nonconforming product. In such cases, trained and authorized personnel should use charts and records to control inventories and prevent inadvertent delivery or use. This may be accomplished electronically by computer control or through use of computer records. Regardless of method, the resulting system should be fail-safe.

Where products are moved immediately by pipeline to the purchaser, the absolute prevention of delivery of nonconforming product may not be practical. In this situation, the purchaser and the supplier should agree on an acceptable system for dealing with nonconformance. The supplier should establish emergency plans for immediately notifying the purchaser when the monitoring system indicates nonconformance and for interrupting the supply if the product is unacceptable to the purchaser. The supplier should also institute a rigorous system for control of the production process. It should include automatic and/or statistical process control of key production process variables that affect product conformance to specifications or requirements. Where appropriate, this would also apply to variables that affect delivery (e.g., pressure, temperature).

This clause of Q91 is identical to clause 4.12 in Q92. Q93 addresses only the identification and segregation portions of this clause in 4.8.

Q91–1987 Standard

4.13.1 Nonconformity Review and Disposition

The responsibility for review and authority for the disposition of nonconforming product shall be defined.

Nonconforming product shall be reviewed in accordance with documented procedures. It may be:

  a) reworked to meet the specified requirements, or

continued

---

continued

b) accepted with or without repair by concession, or

c) re-graded for alternative applications, or

d) rejected or scrapped.

Where required by the contract, the proposed use or repair of product (see 4.13.1 b) which does not conform to specified requirements shall be reported for concession to the purchaser or the purchaser's representative. The description of nonconformity that has been accepted, and of repairs, shall be recorded to denote the actual condition (see 4.16).

Repaired and reworked product shall be re-inspected in accordance with documented procedures.

GUIDANCE

Personnel responsible for review and disposition of nonconforming product should be competent to evaluate the potential effects of disposition or action taken. This will include the effects of reworking, reprocessing, etc., on performance, reliability, safety, esthetics, and other measures.

Documented procedures should define the qualification and training of personnel authorized to disposition nonconforming product. These personnel should have the authority to review product that is non-conforming and make decisions necessary for disposition. Review and disposition shall be in accordance with documented procedures. Records must be maintained of all nonconformities and the disposition made.

Disposition of nonconforming product may include:

1. Reworking to meet specifications or requirements. In the process industry, reworking may include reprocessing or adjusting of mixtures, including blending. These actions should follow established procedures to assure that the resulting product fully complies with specified requirements. This should include testing for conformance to specifications in the same manner as the original material was tested.

2. Accepting with or without reworking, by waiver of specification requirements by the purchaser. When offering nonconforming product for waiver, the supplier should provide a written document describing the nature of the nonconformance(s) and any rework performed.

3. Regrading for alternative applications where product does meet requirements (example, regrading from food to industrial grade).

4. Rejecting or scrapping, which carries the least risk from the purchaser's point of view.

The systems or procedures used for identification, evaluation, segregation, and disposition of nonconforming product must be documented (see clause 4.8).

Records of all nonconformities and their disposition should be maintained with appropriate identification of the lots, items, time periods, production facility, results of all testing or inspections, etc., along with identification of individuals authorizing disposition. These records should contain all information essential to allow auditing of the system and for taking action to prevent recurrence of the nonconformity.

This clause is identical to clause 4.12.1 in Q92. Q93 addresses only the reinspection requirement of this clause in clause 4.8.

4.14 CORRECTIVE ACTION

INTRODUCTION: This clause of the Standard addresses having a documented corrective action system for nonconformances in both product and service areas. It is tied to clause 4.10.3 where an "error signal" has occurred but may be used as part of an overall continuous improvement system. The underlying purpose of this clause is to eliminate the causes of nonconforming products and services by taking preventive action.

Q91–1987 Standard

4.14 Corrective Action

The supplier shall establish, document, and maintain procedures for:

a) investigating the cause of nonconforming product and the corrective action needed to prevent recurrence;

b) analyzing all processes, work operations, concessions, quality records, service reports, and customer complaints to detect and eliminate potential causes of nonconforming product;

GUIDANCE

The objective is to have a documented prevention-based corrective action process from raw material receipt through delivery of product. Documentation should define the system for resolving the nonconformance and verifying effectiveness of corrective action, as well as all required communication pathways. Complaints of nonconformance from purchasers must have documented corrective action. Indications of other quality-related problems that need documented corrective action include: production of nonconforming product or service, complaints from purchasers or internal customers, complaints to sub-contractors, and deficiencies detected during audits or other system reviews and input from individuals involved in the business (see Figure 4.12-1).

A non routine or out-of-control event should result in corrective action, formal acknowledgment of the nonconformance, and written feedback to the purchaser or internal purchaser on corrective actions that have been taken. Response time guidelines for all stages of the corrective action process should be established, and responsibilities and authorities of all affected parties should be defined and understood. Sometimes "emergency" or temporary response actions are required:

- Quarantines, recalls, purchaser alerts, and other measures that prevent use of identified nonconforming product

- Inspection-based actions that identify nonconformances

Emergency (or temporary) actions are needed to prevent use of nonconforming product, but they don't prevent nonconformances from occurring. Preventive actions focus on finding and correcting underlying causes.

For a given nonconformance, emergency (or temporary) action may be necessary while preventive action is being determined. Responsibility and authority for implementing emergency temporary plans should be identified in cases where products for immediate delivery are concerned.

For effective corrective action, all potential causes should be considered. The root causes responsible for the nonconformance should be identified before preventive measures are applied.

Q91–1987 Standard

4.14 Corrective Action

    c) initiating preventative actions to deal with problems to a level corresponding to the risks encountered;

continued

---

continued

d) applying controls to ensure that corrective actions are taken and that they are effective;

GUIDANCE

To prevent recurrence of a nonconformance, it may be necessary to change a design, development, manufacturing, packaging, transit, or storage process, revise a product or service specification, and/or revise the quality system.

Preventive action should be applied to a degree appropriate to the magnitude of potential problems. Safety, purchaser satisfaction, production costs, quality and liability costs, performance, and reliability should all be considered in selecting the appropriate preventive action.

The responsibility and authority for instituting corrective action should be defined as part of the quality system. Coordinating, recording, and monitoring corrective action related to all aspects of the organization or to a particular product should be assigned to a specific function within the organization. The analysis and execution may involve a variety of functions, such as sales, manufacturing, process engineering, and quality assurance (see clause 15.2 of Q94).

Those responsible for taking the corrective actions should be identified for each nonconformance. Sufficient control of process and procedures should be implemented to prevent recurrence of the problem. Progress and completion should be monitored, verified, and documented. The corrective action process should be a subject for management review (see clause 4.1) and for internal quality audits (see clause 4.17).

Q91–1987 Standard

4.14 Corrective Action

e) implementing and recording changes in procedures resulting from corrective action.

GUIDANCE

Permanent changes resulting from corrective action should be recorded in operating procedures, work instructions, manufacturing processes, product specifications, and/or the quality system (see clause 4.5).

This clause in Q91 is identical to clause 4.13 in Q92 and is not covered in Q93.

4.15 HANDLING, STORAGE, PACKAGING, AND DELIVERY

INTRODUCTION: This clause of the Standard applies to finished product, incoming product, and materials in process.

Q91–1987 Standard

4.15.1 General

The supplier shall establish, document, and maintain procedures for handling, storage, packaging, and delivery of product.

GUIDANCE

The requirements of this clause of the Standard are equally applicable to the supplier, all sub-contractors (terminal operator, transporter, distributors, etc.), and purchaser. The distinction between the quality systems needed by each lies in the product-handling functions they perform and the responsibilities they have as defined by contractual agreements relative to the product and delivery process.

Service sub-contractors should be selected based on their ability to meet requirements, including protecting the quality of the product handled (see clause 4.6.2). The supplier should establish and maintain records of quality performance of the service sub-contractor. The type and extent of control applied to a service sub-contractor should be based on records of the sub-contractor's previously demonstrated capability and performance. The supplier should ensure that quality systems at service sub-contractors are effective.

Q91–1987 Standard

4.15.2 Handling

The supplier shall provide methods and means of handling that prevent damage or deterioration.

GUIDANCE

Handling in the chemical and process industries involves many transfers of bulk or packaged product from production through acceptance by the purchaser (see Figure 4.15-1 on page 87).

All means of handling, including the use of pallets, containers, conveyors, vessels, tanks, pipelines, and vehicles, are to be addressed in the supplier's system.

The supplier should ensure that product is handled so that product quality is maintained. Documented procedures should govern product as it moves through the handling operation to ensure that:

- Product is not inadvertently mixed

- Contamination does not occur

- Product is protected from change other than normal aging

- Product does not miss a required operation or inspection

Handling procedures should assure that the potential for contamination, reaction, and/or degradation is minimized or eliminated. Packages or other containers should be inspected before product filling/loading to assure the integrity of the container and the absence of manufacturing residues, contaminants, or other foreign material. Sampling of dedicated containers may be required to determine if the "heel" will contaminate incoming product.

Pipeline and loading systems should be dedicated to specific products and positively isolated from all sources of contamination. If not dedicated, special changeover or line clearing procedures are required to assure that product quality is maintained when header systems or shared loading and transfer systems are employed.

Methods for product identification (records and/or labeling, where appropriate) should provide durable information for traceability throughout all handling processes to delivery at the purchaser.

A lot should be segregated before testing and not commingled with other production. During transfer of contents of a rundown, bulk storage, or shipping tank to smaller containers, the larger vessel should be thoroughly mixed and totally isolated from any streams or input which might change the quality of that lot.

All interruptions to loading/filling of a bulk product should be documented in production records for later use in process control and problem resolution. If the loading/filling operation of a bulk product is significantly interrupted on either a planned or unplanned basis, then samples should be taken and tested to determine if the product still conforms to specifications. The need to resample and retest should be based on the characteristics of the specific product and the specific loading/filling process.

Q91–1987 Standard

4.15.3 Storage

The supplier shall provide secure storage areas or stock rooms to prevent damage or deterioration of product, pending use, or delivery. Appropriate methods for authorizing receipt and the dispatch to and from such areas shall be stipulated. In order to detect deterioration, the condition of product in stock shall be assessed at appropriate intervals.

GUIDANCE

The supplier needs to ensure that product is stored under conditions that do not deteriorate or change the quality of the product beyond normal aging. Maintenance procedures for storage vessels should address the potential for environmental contamination.

Storage containers should be selected with consideration given to:

- Materials of construction

- Pressure rating

- Storage temperature

- Storage capacity

- Corrosion

- Contamination potential

- Previous contents

- Loading facilities

- Product characteristics

Procedures should be documented for receipt, transfer, and changing production or service of storage containers from one product to another.

Products in storage need to be checked periodically to detect possible deterioration. Rotation of stock and shelf-life need to be considered in storage procedures. Products with limited shelf-life or requiring special protection during transport or storage should be identified and procedures maintained to ensure deteriorated products are not put into use (see clause 4.13).

Q91–1987 Standard

4.15.4 Packaging

The supplier shall control packing, preservation, and marking processes (including materials used) to the extent necessary to ensure conformance to specified requirements and shall identify, preserve, and segregate all product from the time of receipt until the supplier's responsibility ceases.

GUIDANCE

A "package" is any container or apparatus in which or through which a product is transported or stored, including tank cars, hopper cars, trucks, bags, bulk bags, drums, boxes, pipelines, tanks, and barges.

The specific package should be carefully selected. Considerations include potential for corrosion and deterioration as well as previous contents, loading and unloading facilities, and product characteristics.

Procedures should be defined and documented to ensure that quality is maintained during packaging. Package cleanliness, to prevent possible contamination, and package integrity, to prevent possible loss and injury, must be addressed. Inspection plans and responsibilities of the product manufacturer, package sub-contractor, and transporter should be documented and communicated.

Dedicated containers may reduce some quality concerns while raising others. Use of dedicated containers requires careful planning and implementation.

In instances where weighing of product is impractical, such as bulk transport in ships or barges, procedures should be developed to accurately measure quantities by other means.

Packages should be labeled or documented, according to the specifications and applicable regulations (see clause 4.8). Marking and labeling should be legible and durable.

Containers that cannot be physically marked, such as rail cars, trucks, and other bulk containers, should be uniquely identified on records such as bills of lading and the certificate of analysis. They should be placarded to meet safety requirements.

Q91–1987 Standard

4.15.5 Delivery

The supplier shall arrange for the protection of the quality of product after final inspection and test. Where contractually specified, this protection shall be extended to include delivery to destination.

GUIDANCE

Transporters include trucking agencies, pipeline operators, shipping agencies, terminal operators, and freight forwarders. The contract should specify the extent to which the supplier transporter, sub-contractor, and purchaser are obligated to protect product quality during delivery.

Provision for protecting product quality is important during all phases of delivery. Consider the various methods of delivery and variations in environmental conditions that may be encountered during delivery. The purchaser should ensure that unloading procedures, equipment, lines, and storage will not jeopardize product integrity.

For time-sensitive products, including services, delivery time is a critical factor. When this is the case, procedures must ensure acceptable delivery time.

Avoid in-transit product transfers during bulk product shipments.

Contamination, damage, and loss are risks of in-transit product transfers. If an emergency situation leads to a transfer, the responsible carrier or terminal must receive clear and complete transfer instructions from the supplier. (Note: In-transit transfers of "less-than-truckload" [LTL] shipments of packaged goods are common and acceptable practice.)

If product (or the container) is damaged or exposed to potential contamination, contact the supplier immediately. Under no circumstances should spilled or damaged product be repackaged and delivered to the purchaser without proper authority (see clause 4.13).

For common carriers, unless specified differently in the contract, the purchaser is responsible for protecting product quality when the purchaser has arranged the shipment. Although the purchaser may be paying for the common carrier, the supplier has responsibility for protecting product quality when the supplier arranges the shipment.

Pipeline transfers of product directly to purchasers present unique quality control situations. Quality of product should be monitored with methods and frequencies agreed upon by the purchaser and the supplier. All inputs to pipelines should be well identified. The quality of each input should be monitored on a basis agreed upon with the purchasers.

If multiple suppliers use common pipelines, effective common procedures for quality assurances must be documented and used by all product suppliers, pipeline subcontractors, and purchasers. Compliance to these procedures should be audited.

The requirements of clause 4.15 of Q91 are identical to clause 4.14 of Q92. This clause does not apply to Q93.

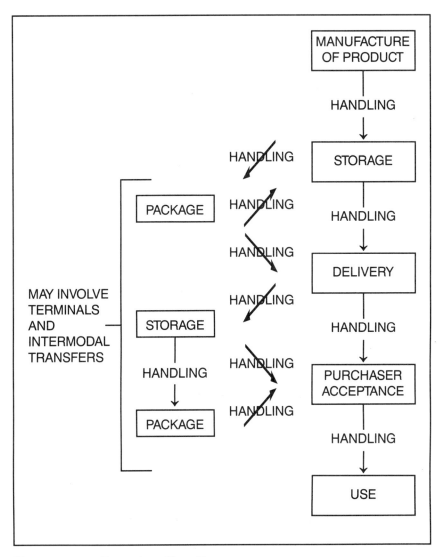

Figure 4.15-1 Examples of handling

4.16 QUALITY RECORDS

INTRODUCTION: This clause of the Standard discusses the record-keeping system needed to meet purchaser requirements.

Q91–1987 Standard

4.16 Quality Records

The supplier shall establish and maintain procedures for identification, collection, indexing, filing, storage, maintenance, and disposition of quality records.

Quality records shall be maintained to demonstrate achievement of the required quality and the effective operation of the quality system. Pertinent sub-contractor quality records shall be an element of these data.

continued

---

continued

All quality records shall be legible and identifiable to the product involved. Quality records shall be stored and maintained in such a way that they are readily retrievable in facilities that provide a suitable environment to minimize deterioration or damage and to prevent loss. Retention times of quality records shall be established and recorded. Where agreed contractually, quality records shall be made available for evaluation by the purchaser or the purchaser's representative for an agreed period.

GUIDANCE

The supplier should maintain adequate records to demonstrate achievement of the required quality and to verify effective operation of the supplier's quality system. The supplier may choose more than one medium (e.g., paper, electronic, or microfilm) for record storage. The method must provide timely retrieval of records and security from unauthorized access. Whatever medium is selected, the records should be protected from loss, damage, and deterioration due to environmental conditions. Document the procedures for all aspects of record maintenance.

The supplier should define the types of quality records that need to be kept. The following types of records are specifically referred to in this Standard:

- Management reviews (clause 4.1.3)

- Contract reviews (clause 4.3)

- Design reviews (clause 4.4.5 a)

- Acceptable sub-contractors (clause 4.6.2)

- Purchaser supplied product (clause 4.7)

- Product identification and traceability (clause 4.8)

- Qualified process equipment and personnel (clause 4.9.2)

- Receiving inspection and testing (clause 4.10.1)

- Inspection and test records (clause 4.10.4)

- Calibration and measurement assurance records (clause 4.11 f)

- Test hardware checks (clause 4.11)

- Inspection and test status (clause 4.12)

- Nonconformity review and disposition (clause 4.14)

- Training records (clause 4.18)

The supplier should set retention times for quality records appropriate to the type of record. Retention times should be documented (see clause 4.5). Consider these factors in setting retention times:

- Requirements of the contract with the purchaser

- Applicable regulatory requirements (e.g., FDA)

- The stated useful life of the purchaser's product

- The final sale of the supplier's product

Process data are increasingly recorded by on-line computer systems in the chemical industry. If these records are used as part of the quality system, the supplier should:

- Verify that software meets the quality system needs

- Verify the accuracy and precision of recorded values

- Screen the records for missing or wild observations

- Protect old records from being written over by new records

- Create archives of electronic records to assure recovery when required

Clause 4.16 in Q91 is identical to clause 4.15 in Q92. Clause 4.10 in Q93 addresses only inspection and test records required to substantiate conformance with specified requirements.

4.17 INTERNAL QUALITY AUDITS

INTRODUCTION: This clause of the Standard states that internal quality system audits are essential to maintain the quality system. A quality audit is the principal source (see clause 4.1.2.2) of answers to three critical questions:

- Are all the detailed provisions of the quality system being carried out as intended?

- Is the quality system effective in producing the specified quality results?

- Does the quality system conform to all external requirements that apply to it, such as purchasers' contracts, applicable quality system standards, and government regulations, in addition to the supplier's internal policies and plans?

By focusing on the system, quality audits differ from quality control, which focuses on the decision to accept or reject products, intermediates, or raw materials. Quality system audits also differ from management reviews, which review audit reports along with other sources of information to determine how well the quality system is functioning and to initiate any needed changes.

While this clause of the Standard does not exclude product and process audits, quality systems audits are the minimum requirement for compliance with Q91.

Q91–1987 Standard

4.17 Internal Quality Audits

The supplier shall carry out a comprehensive system of planned and documented internal quality audits to verify whether quality activities comply with planned arrangements and to determine the effectiveness of the quality system.

Audits shall be scheduled on the basis of the status and importance of the activity.

The audits and follow-up actions shall be carried out in accordance with documented procedures.

The results of the audits shall be documented and brought to the attention of the personnel having responsibility in the area audited. The management personnel responsible for the area shall take timely corrective action on the deficiencies found by the audit (see 4.1.3).

GUIDANCE

An internal quality system audit function begins with a management policy describing its scope, responsibility, and authority, and requiring auditees (audited areas) to cooperate during audits and to carry out corrective actions.

There should be written procedures for planning, carrying out, reporting, documenting, and following up audits, and also for selecting, training, and qualifying auditors.

All activities within the quality system should be audited. Prioritize activities by considering:

- How critical they are to the quality of the product

- The results of previous audits

• How difficult the activities are to keep in control

There should be a schedule of periodic audits that reflects the priorities; in the absence of other information, audits are usually conducted annually.

The lead auditor should be familiar with the standards that apply to the supplier's business. The specific clause to be audited and questions to be answered are determined on the basis of relevant standards, the quality manual, and the history of the auditee.

Members of an audit team should have the necessary qualifications and experience to fulfill their roles on the team. The lead auditors should be independent from the area being audited.

The team collects evidence during the audit, focusing on procedures, work instructions and records, the facility and equipment, and observation of work being performed. The evidence should show both what is working as intended and what needs to be corrected. An audit concludes with a meeting with the auditee's senior management, at which the lead auditor presents audit observations and overall conclusions regarding the quality system.

The formal written report should include the audit date and location, conclusions regarding the quality system's effectiveness and its conformance with relevant standards, and any deficiencies found. The team should give the report to senior management having authority and responsibility to take corrective action and to the auditee's management.

The auditee is responsible for determining and carrying out actions to correct the deficiencies. Usually the goal is to identify actions that will eliminate the cause of deficiencies and thus prevent their recurrence. The time to complete the actions is agreed to by senior management and the auditee in consultation with the auditors.

Management, with the cooperation of the audit team, should follow up to verify and document that corrections have been completed on time and are effective.

For more information, see, for example, *ISO 10011, Guidelines for Auditing Quality Systems.*

Clause 4.16 in Q91 is identical to clause 4.15 in Q92. This subject is not mentioned in Q93.

4.18 TRAINING

INTRODUCTION: This clause of the Standard deals with the way a supplier manages its employee training program.

Q91–1987 Standard

4.18 Training

The supplier shall establish and maintain procedures for identifying the training needs and provide for the training of all personnel performing activities affecting quality. Personnel performing specific assigned tasks shall be qualified on the basis of appropriate education, training, and/or experience, as required. Appropriate records of training shall be maintained (see 4.16).

GUIDANCE

All employees who affect the quality of the suppliers' product and services or who interact with the purchaser need proper training. For example, this requirement would apply to quality auditing and order processing employees.

The training program should:

- Determine the training needs of all employees who affect the quality of the supplier's products and services.

- Arrange for the required training for these employees.

- Qualify personnel against job requirements.

- Maintain records demonstrating that employees have achieved the training and requirements for their job responsibility.

The elements of the training program should be documented (see clause 4.16), including:

- The content of the training activity

- Instructor identification and qualifications to teach assigned courses or skills

- Employee training completion records

Training course content should be linked to standard operating procedures and overall documentation of the quality system. The quality system should require specific employee training. Standard operating procedures and work instructions should state specific training and/or skill levels required for operating personnel assigned to specific activities.

The training recommendations for Q94 (see clause 18.1) should also be considered. These recommendations cover all levels of employees.

Executives and managers need to understand the quality system and its tools and techniques so they can evaluate the effectiveness of the quality system.

Technical personnel, including those in marketing, finance, procurement, and process and product engineering, should be trained to enhance their contribution to the success of the quality system. Give particular attention to training in statistical techniques. In the CPI, technical personnel would include those in the research and development function, pilot plant operations, and control and analytical laboratories.

All production supervisors and operators should be thoroughly trained in how to do their jobs. They should understand the relationship of their duties to quality and safety. Production supervisors and operators in the CPI should understand how they affect the process, the logic behind set points and process control ranges, and the effect on final product quality of being outside the specified control ranges for process control readings.

Some operators may require certification of their skills. This would apply to craftsmen (e.g., welders, electricians, and pipefitters) as well as operators in particular plant areas (i.e., in the waste treatment plant).

This clause 4.18 of Q91 is similar to clause 4.17 in Q92. Clause 4.11 in Q93 addresses only final inspection and testing training.

4.19 SERVICING

INTRODUCTION: This clause of the Standard covers all aspects of "service after the sale" that are defined in the purchaser's contract.

Q91–1987 Standard

4.19 Servicing

Where servicing is specified in the contract, the supplier shall establish and maintain procedures for performing and verifying that servicing meets the specified requirements.

GUIDANCE

The clause does not refer to the normal service/technical assistance activities by the supplier that are common business practices, or to the provision of a service, unless *specified in a contract*. Contractual requirements for "servicing" define the supplier's responsibility to help the purchaser ensure proper use of the product following delivery. Servicing means repair, maintenance, upgrading, etc., in the hard goods or mechanical industries. In the chemical and process industries, servicing occurs where there is an ongoing relationship between the supplier and purchaser relating to the performance of the product. Examples might include water treatment, catalyst supply, and licensing of technology.

Required servicing should be documented in a plan agreed to by the supplier and purchaser. This document should clearly outline the responsibilities among supplier, purchaser, and any third parties. It should also provide for regular reviews to verify that the service provided meets the requirements of the contract. The document may refer to:

- Specialized handling and test equipment needed, and the maintenance and control of it

- How the purchaser's complaints are to be resolved

- A performance specification for the product or service

- The particular operating, control, inspection, and testing procedures used to verify the performance of the service

- Back-up provisions including technical assistance and the availability of alternate equipment or materials

- Training and qualification of appropriate purchaser personnel

- The planning of service activities

- How to contact supplier's personnel in case of emergency

This clause of Q91 requires the supplier to establish and maintain procedures describing how to perform and verify the specified servicing. This clause of the Standard does not apply to Q92 or Q93.

4.20 STATISTICAL TECHNIQUES

INTRODUCTION: This clause of the Standard addresses the use of statistical tools for determining and expressing the level of confidence in the quality of the supplier's product and service. It addresses the basis for collecting and using data to make good quality decisions.

Q91–1987 Standard

4.20 Statistical Techniques

Where appropriate, the supplier shall establish procedures for identifying adequate statistical techniques required for verifying the acceptability of process capability and product characteristics

---

GUIDANCE

The supplier should have the resources to:

- Determine where statistical techniques are applicable and useful

- Determine appropriate techniques for use

- Implement their use where needed

The supplier should establish procedures for verifying the acceptability of process capability for key product characteristics. Statistical techniques should be used to monitor and control process operations and product quality.
Statistical techniques may be used to:

- Assess sub-contractor acceptability (clause 4.6.2)

- Determine process capability (clause 4.9)

- Assess measurement capability (clause 4.2 d, 4.11)

- Monitor key process and product characteristics (clause 4.10)

- Investigate nonconformities (clause 4.14)

- Identify improvement opportunities (clauses 4.14, 4.17)

- Forecast production requirements and scheduling plans (clause 4.13)

- Evaluate customer complaints (clause 4.14)

- Determine sampling methodology (clause 4.11)

Statistical techniques include:

- Histograms

- Scatter plots

- Control charts

- Run charts

- Statistical design of experiments

- Analysis of Variance

GLOSSARY

CAS number: A number assigned by the Chemical Abstracts Service of the American Chemical Society to identify a chemical

Inspection: Performing activities such as measuring, examining, testing, or gauging one or more characteristics of a product or service, and comparing these with specified requirements to determine conformity. Note: The term *requirements* sometimes is used broadly to include subjective yet required standards of good workmanship.

Intermediate: A definable quantity of material, the result of a process, which is capable of being isolated (in space or time) and subjected to quality testing for evidence that the overall product or process remains in control

Lot: A definite quantity of a product or material accumulated under conditions considered uniform for sampling purposes. For a continuous process, a lot is usually defined by a time interval. For a batch process, each batch can be considered a lot. If parts of a lot are later stored and/or shipped under significantly different conditions, it may be necessary to define each part as a separate lot. This definition is based on the broad definition of a process as being any activity that changes the physical or chemical properties used to define the product—blending, mixing, packaging under different conditions, and so on—as well as the usual production processes.

Procedure: Descriptions of activities critical to the maintenance of quality, describing with whom, with what, when, where, and how an activity is carried out

Product: Material or service produced by the supplier for sale to a purchaser

Purchased product: Material or services purchased from a sub-contractor for use in the supplier's process

Purchaser: The company that is buying the supplier's products or services. The purchaser is the supplier's customer. The purchaser chooses the quality system requirements that the supplier's quality assurance system needs to satisfy.

Quality plan: A document, specific to each product (or group of similar products), that sets out the quality-related activities for that product. A quality plan should include references to raw material specification and quality control procedures, product formulation, process control, intermediate and finished product specifications and quality control procedures, sampling procedures and packaging specifications, and any other relevant procedures. A quality plan might form part of a detailed operating procedure.

Service: The tangible or intangible result of activities or processes, such as a computer program, a design, directions for use, or the execution of a toll production process

Sub-Contractor: Any provider of purchased products (e.g., raw materials, in-bound goods or services, utilities, or equipment) or services that come into the supplier's company (organization, plant, or process). Toll converters, contract warehouses, outside laboratories, packagers, and repackagers are all examples of sub-contractors, whether internal or external. Operations internal to a supplier's company may be regarded as sub-contractors if they are outside of the quality system defined by the supplier.

Supplier: The company (organization, plant, or process) that is establishing a quality assurance system and producing the product or service covered by the standard. Very often you, as the user of this guide, will be the supplier.

Testing: Determining the capability of an item to meet specified requirements by subjecting the item to a set of physical, chemical, environmental, or operating actions and conditions

Verification: Reviewing, inspecting, testing, checking, auditing, or otherwise establishing and documenting whether items, processes, services, or documents conform to specified requirements

Work instruction: A document that tells *how* to do something rather than when, where, or with whom; a detailed step-by-step description of a work activity

INDEX